Design and Build Modern Datacentres, A to Z practical guide

Engineer Said AL Hosni

Published by Engineer Said AL Hosni, 2021.

While every precaution has been taken in the preparation of this book, the publisher assumes no responsibility for errors or omissions, or for damages resulting from the use of the information contained herein.

DESIGN AND BUILD MODERN DATACENTRES, A TO Z PRACTICAL GUIDE

First edition. January 1, 2021.

Copyright © 2021 Engineer Said AL Hosni.

ISBN: 979-8224311095

Written by Engineer Said AL Hosni.

Table of Contents

DESIGN AND BUILD MODERN DATACENTRES

A to Z practical guide

ENGINEER SAID AL HOSNI

Design and Build Modern Datacentres
A to Z practical guide

Engineer Said Al Hosni
Sultanate of Oman, Muscat

Said@majantec.com (**Email**)
www.majantec.com (**Website**)

First published, 2020

Copyright © 2020 by Engineer Said Al Hosni. All Rights Reserved.

Acknowledgements

I am very grateful to my family, who has always been supportive of me during my technical research and my great preoccupation while writing this book. I am also thankful to my friend, Dr Khaled Al-Rawahi, who has helped me with his valuable feedback.

I cannot forget my previous employers, who inspired me during the twenty-seven years of works, which gained me a valuable experience throughout those projects I completed during those years.

Also, special thanks to those who contributed to the completion of this book, even with a word of encouragement. It has had an impact on my motivation to accomplish this book.

Dedication

To the souls of my dear mom and dad, even though you did not witness this moment with me, I am sure that you are blessing this step wherever you are. To my beautiful family, who has always supported me to reach my aspirations, you have always been the best support in my long, arduous path. All my appreciation to everyone who supported me for getting this work done.

Preface

Congratulations on finding out about this book. I am writing this book to help Datacentre owners and designers learn how to design and build Datacentre correctly.

This book is one of the rare books designed to simplify the complexity and guide the learner to explore and discover the secrets of Datacentre designs. I hope the information in this book is intuitive enough for Datacentre designers to follow through with clear guidance. Having a good foundation of IT skills will help a lot in understanding this book.

This book is an excellent opportunity to understand and practice Datacentre designing and building. It is an essence of my thoughts and experiences during 29 years of work in the field of information technology, particularly designing and building of Datacentres.

My goal in this book is to fill in the noticeable shortage in books that deal with the design of Datacentres systematically. This book covers the designing and building of Datacentres, from the stage of site selection to the stage of completing the construction and operation.

I can guarantee that anyone familiar with IT and projects management will be able to design and build a Datacentre according to the latest specifications by reading and understanding this book.

Chapter 1: What is a Datacentre?

Definition of Datacentre

A Datacentre is a building or dedicated space within a building or a group of buildings that are used to host computer systems and related associated components such as telecommunications and storage systems.

THE ENVIRONMENT OF these buildings is highly controlled by temperature, humidity and electricity power, access authorisation, and monitoring.

A DATACENTRE IS THE heart of any institution. It is where the business of any kind depends heavily on for information systems processing, storage and retrieval of data. This means that institutions depend highly on IT for their business, bringing about a situation where they do not bear interruption of this service in any way. However, IT admins have to pay attention to this aspect.

Why Do We Need a Datacentre?

Institutions need Datacentres for several reasons. We can summarise these reasons as the following:

1. Data becomes the most valuable asset for any enterprise (Big Data).

2. Enterprise becomes a data-hungry species.

3. Demand for more processing power is increasing.

4. Data theft becomes more dangerous than ever.

5. The need to guarantee information security is essential for the enterprise.

Is it Recommended to Build a Datacentre or Rent a Space in an Existing one (Outsourcing)?

Typically, building a Datacentre is essential for large enterprises or enterprises that believe their data is of paramount importance, such as Defence and law enforcers. This option is the most costly, and it requires a considerable budget, perfect design, good management teams and perfect supportive contractors, and active suppliers and utility providers.

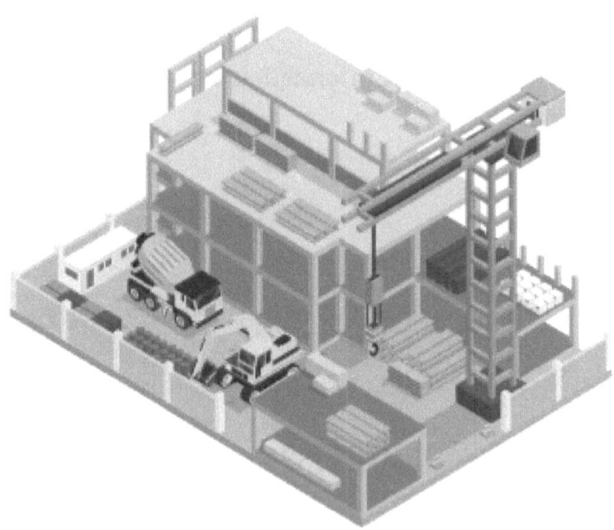

Advantages of Datacentre Outsourcing

• Guaranteed Uptime

Usually, the service provider has at least TIER 3 Datacentre along with one or more backup Datacentre that guarantees little chance for downtime and fast recovery in case of disaster. Also, the customers are usually protected by a Service Level Agreement (SLA) that guarantees their rights.

• Higher Scalability

It is much smoother for the customer to acquire more space or processing as needed with reasonable cost and without excessive planning for upgrade compared with own Datacentre.

• Better Flexibility and Speed

It is much flexible and fast to get the service compared to building your Datacentre. With this option, you can choose the best service provider and a suitable plan, and then you are ready to go.

• Cost Savings

THIS OPTION CAN SAVE the customer a considerable amount of money, as he/she is not responsible for building, running cost, and utility bills (the hardware and the upgrade cost except the colocation service).

• Improved Latency and Connectivity

The service provider provides the best available network connectivity typically as they are providing the IT services to multiple customers. Therefore, it is very worthwhile for them to hire a high bandwidth from the communication companies, and this helps the customers to enjoy minimum latency communication.

- **Increased Business Focus**

Outsourcing allows the customers to focus on business rather than monitoring, testing, auditing, maintaining and upgrading the Datacentre.

Disadvantages of Datacentre Outsourcing

◇ Possibility of Unpleasant Surprises

The customer must understand the contract very well before going on outsourcing. This is because the service providers vary in the type of provided services, uptime percentage, Recovery Time Objective (RTO) and Recovery Point Objective (RPO), backup type, terms and conditions, and ownership of data and termination period.

Understanding these aspects is essential for the customer, and usually, there should be SLA to facilitate the relationship between the service provider and the customer.

◇ Data Security

Despite all pledges and contracts, there is always an opportunity for the server administrator to access your data, especially in the case of managed services Datacentres. Therefore, these services are usually not recommended for Defence, law enforcement and police.

◇ Loss of Control

There is always a chance of loss of control on your remote services, for example, in case of the local enterprise Datacentre, you might ask your employees to provide you with any customised data reports immediately. For you to achieve this in remote managed services, you need to have third-party support, which can take longer time based on the load on the service provider employees, and this might also cost you much.

And in the case of internet failure, the connectivity with the data is lost until the service is restored, which is unlikely to happen with your local enterprise Datacentre.

◈ Vendor Lock-In

In managed services, you might find yourself stuck with a specific vendor as your current service provider systems are built on that vendor and it might be risky for you to move to another service provider. Therefore, you must understand the contract very well to make sure you can quickly move to another service provider with minimal downtime and switching cost regardless of the hardware/software vendor of the second service provider.

⎯⎯◉⎯⎯

TIP : *Building a private Datacentre for an institution is recommended if the organization is financially prepared and has a qualified workforce to operate the Datacentre.*

Types of Datacentre Outsourcing

Colocation (COLO): Leasing space, power and bandwidth from a Datacentre provider. In this service, the service provider is responsible for the infrastructure such as redundant power and redundant cooling, networking, and physical security. The clients have to provide the servers and storage; they have control of their servers. The service provider never interferes in the configuration of the servers and the clients have the freedom to manage their infrastructure using their own team. In some situations, the clients can hire an area protected with a cage, and nobody can access the area without their approval unless there is an emergency.

HOSTING: Leasing storage and computing resources on a server that is managed by a third party. Cloud falls into this category. In this option, the client can use a ready-made environment for their processing and storage; this is an easy option and fast existence choice.

MANAGED SERVICES: Usually, the operational management of your Datacentre infrastructure across the network, server, and storage. The idea of managed services is that you hire the service for monthly lease, where the service provider tries their best to offer you a stable and efficient service, and minimise problems as this allows them to make a good profit. This service provides you with peace of mind, as you have complete virtual IT departments that serve your needs and take care of upgrades and licencing headache. Therefore, you don't need IT experts as these departments take care of all the client issues. The service provider does their best to be proactive and discover and find solutions to the problems before it happens.

Types of Cloud Computing Services

1. Software as a Service (SaaS)

It is a software distribution model in which a third-party provider hosts applications and makes them available to prospective customers over the internet.

2. Platform as a Service (PaaS)

It is a cloud-computing model in which cloud vendors provide developers with a platform for building apps.

3. Infrastructure as a service (IaaS)

It is a cloud computing that provides virtualised computing resources over the internet.

4. Desktop as a Service (DaaS)

It is a form of cloud computing service where the service provider provides a virtual desktop to end users over the internet, and the license is for each user's subscription.

Where Should I Build my Datacentre?

Datacentres are one of the most critical business assets. They are one of the buildings with a high construction cost, and they also drain much money to be maintained correctly. Still, they are considered the beating heart of the institution. Therefore, they must be designed correctly and with special care, and to do this, the following points must be obeyed:

1. Avoid natural disaster area.

You have to study the location for the last 100 years, to find out whether it is affected by flooding, tornadoes or high winds. It is also essential to choose a place that is away from high temperature and fire sources as it can cause a disaster.

2. Choose a place higher than sea level

It is recommended to build the Datacentre at a location that is 20 metres above the sea level; this is a necessary precaution to avoid floods of any type.

3. Avoid highway roads

Always choose a location that is at least 800 metres away from any highway road. This is to avoid any accidents that might harm the Datacentre. The main roads can also generate vibrations that adversely affect the Datacentre.

4. Avoid airline paths

For safety reasons, it is crucial to choose a location that is away from airline paths.

5. Avoid electromagnetic interference

Always choose a location that is at least 400 metres away from any airport or satellite centre.

6. Avoid vibrations

The Datacentre should be away from any vibration sources such as railway or manufacturing entity.

7. Away from military base

Always choose a location that is at least 800 metres away from any military base.

8. Away from the foreign embassy

The building must not be located adjacent to a foreign embassy.

9. Electromagnetic Compatibility (EMC)

Risks must be minimised by locating away from radar transmitters and mobile phone masts.

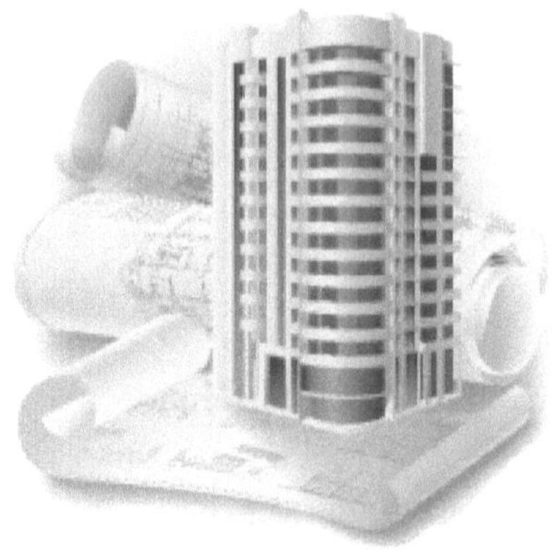

Additional Essential Requirements

1. Secured location

The Datacentre must be adequately secured, and the location plays an essential part in ensuring that the building and the surrounding area is secured. Hence, the location shouldn't be closed to country borders or hazardous areas.

2. Soil suitability

The soil must be examined to find out whether it can hold a massive building or it requires special treatment before building the Datacentre.

3. Power availability

Datacentre requires a tremendous amount of power. Therefore, you need to make sure that you have enough power sources in the location, and if you plan for TIER 4 Datacentre, make sure that you can get power from two independent power grids.

4. Internet connectivity

Internet is essential for Datacentre day-to-day activity; therefore, ensure the availability of reliable internet service.

5. Weather

Always select the coldest location for your Datacentre, as this reduces the cost of cooling, which is usually one of the highest running cost.

6. Future expansion

Although Datacentres designers keen on designing Datacentres as expandable building, no one knows the future needs. Hence, make sure that there is enough free area for future expansion.

7. Location accessibility

The Datacentre should be built in a location where it can be reached quickly by the employees and suppliers, as this reduces the transport cost for the employees and company. The police and fire department needs to enter the place with ease when required.

8. Location proximity

Public transport is essential for the employees; this is because the working time in the Datacentre is 24 hours, so the employees change shifts continuously, and the shift can be changed at night where the employees need easy access to the public transport.

It is essential to build the Datacentre in a location where it is easy to get all of the required services and easy for suppliers to reach.

9. Quality of life

When choosing the Datacentre location, you must think of the required needs by the employees such as groceries, restaurants and entertainment centres.

TIP : *Some may think that the required precautions when choosing a Datacentre construction site are exaggerated but be confident that these precautions are very necessary.*

How Big Does the Datacentre Need to Be?

To decide the size of the required Datacentre, you need to consider the following:

1. The number of servers you want to put into the Datacentre

Before you decide to build a Datacentre, you need to know the number of servers you will need, and this can be determined by the services you plan to offer with the Datacentre.

2. The server types you plan to use

You need to decide which server type you plan to use, whether cabinet-mounted, blade or any other kind. The server type affects the amount of required power and cooling, along with the white space required.

3. Do you consider virtualisation?

It is also essential to know if you plan to use virtualisation because if so, then you might need less space and number of cabinets.

4. The amount of electrical power you can source at the location

The size of the Datacentre is directly proportional to the available electric power sources. Therefore, you cannot build a Datacentre that needs more energy than the available energy in the area you want to build the Datacentre.

5. Your expansion percentage plan

You need to decide the expected percentage of future expansion to design a scalable/expandable Datacentre that can serve for many years.

***

TIP : *One of the most frequent challenges of Datacentre future expansion is the lack of space and the lack of required services, such as electricity, cooling and network.*

What Tier or Class of Datacentre do I Need?

Datacentres are categorised by Tiers, namely Tier 1 to 4. This tiering is based on the amount of downtime during a year and considers electricity availability only. It is categorised by Uptime Institute, as shown in the table below:

Datacentre tiers

Tier	Availability %	Annual Downtime
Tier1	99.671%(No redundancy)	28.8 hours
Tier2	99.749%(Partial Redundancy)	22 Hours
Tier3	99.982%(N+1 fault-tolerant)	1.6 Hours
Tier4	99.995%(2N+1 fully redundant)	26.3 minutes

How Should an Organisation Select the Right Tier?

Choosing the required tier for the Datacentre depends on the actual need to ensure the level of business continuity. For service providers, Tier IV or Tier III is a prerequisite to compete with other competitors and to attract customers.

AS FOR THE INDEPENDENT institutions, they need to balance between the actual needs and the available resources. If the data is very critical and there is no backup, then going for anything below Tier III is not recommended. But in the case of availability of multiple Datacentres linked together, then Tier II or Tier I for tiny branches is reasonable.

The most common definition of the four levels can be summarised as follows:

Tier I Tactical: This tier has one path for power and cooling, and a few redundant and backup components.

———◉———

TIER II Tactical: It has a single path for electrical power and cooling system with some redundant components and backups.

———◉———

TIER III Strategic: This tier has multiple paths for electric power and cooling systems so that maintenance, upgrades and updates can take place without taking the Datacentre offline.

———◉———

TIER IV Strategic: This tier has completely fault-tolerant with full redundancy for every component.

What Power Capacity Do You Need?

To find out the required power capacity for the Datacentre, you need to know the following:

1. White space area

The white space area is the room where the server cabinets are placed, and this is one of the vital factors used in the power calculation equation.

2. The expected density per cabinet

You have to decide the density of the cabinet as it can be full, half or low density. This allows you to calculate the required future load. However, cabinets are usually estimated as full density, where most of the Datacentres starts with low or half density. Designing it as full density is helpful for the future as you can use it as full density without any risk.

3. Total of existence and future cabinets

The number of existence cabinets along with the future expected cabinets are required to be able to calculate the required cooling and the IT load power along with other services that required power, to come out with the amount of critical and uncritical service power requirements.

4. The expected required power for each cabinet

The expected required power for each cabinet is considered by the cabinet density, so you have to decide the expected density.

5. The required cooling capacity

Usually, the cooling capacity is calculated based on the number of cabinets and the cabinet's density, and the cooling calculation differs between DX cooling and chilled water cooling system.

6. Other supporting systems

Other supporting systems in the Datacentre have to be calculated, such as lighting. Lighting is calculated based on the area, CCTV system, access control system, VESDA and firefighting systems, etc.

What is a Suitable Building Layout?

There are many suitable layouts for Datacentres, and you can choose the one that suits you, which can be fully ground floor or multi-floor building. In all cases, some essential specifications need to be considered while designing the Datacentre.

YOU SHOULD BEAR IN mind that designing and building a Datacentre is an independent knowledge by itself; it is not an ordinary building that any civil engineer can do. Therefore, you can't merely ask an ordinary building designer to design you a Datacentre without having a proficient Datacentre consultant; otherwise, the result might be disastrous.

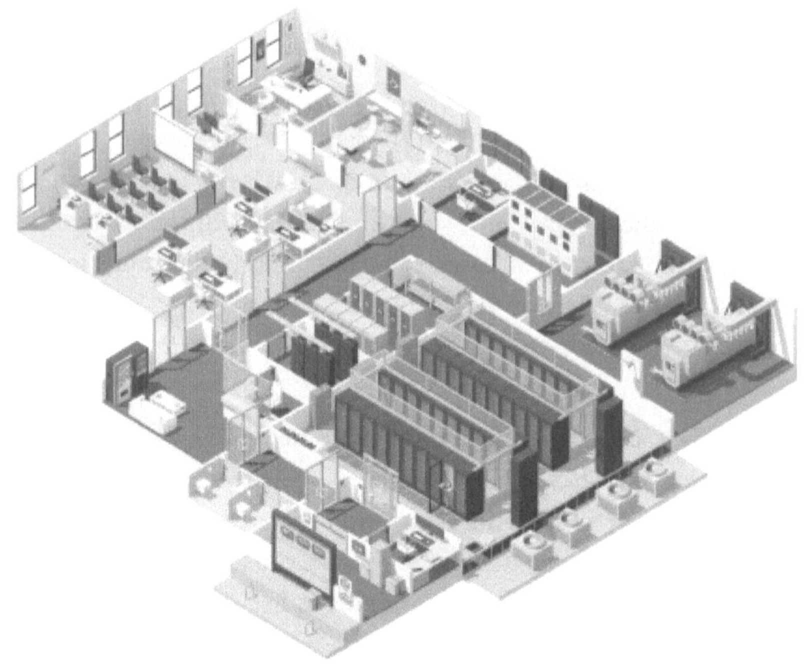

Sample of typical Datacentre layout

TIP : *One of the most significant catastrophic errors when designing Datacentres is to assign the design matter to an engineer who is not specialised in designing Datacentres.*

Average Datacentre Construction Cost

The table below displays the approximate percentage cost distributed among the main Datacentre components.

Cost Line Item	Percentage of the project total %
1. Excavation and backfilling	0.1
2. General construction	**14.7**
3. Access floor system	0.8
4. Ceiling systems	0.4
5. Wall finishes	0.4
6. Floor finishes	0.9
7. Structural steel	3.1
8. Fire protection system	**4.4**
9. Plumbing systems	0.4
10. Mechanical systems	**14.4**
11. Electrical systems	**28.3**
12. Monitoring and security systems	8.0
13. General conditions	2.2
14. General contractor fee	1.6
15. Permits	0.1
16. Construction management fee	1.8
17. Design fee	0.9
18. Consultation fees	**4.5**
19. Project Management	**13.0**

Note: The above table is an approximate percentage; it can differ from country to another.

Chapter 2: Datacentre Building Requirements

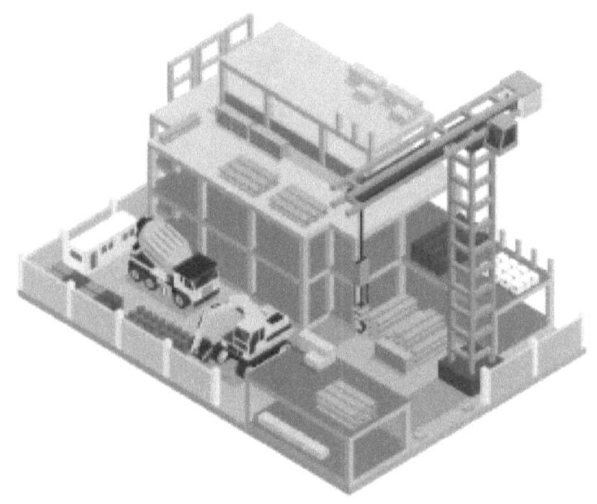

Datacentre Key Components

Datacentre key components are the building, electrical systems, mechanical systems, security and safety systems, monitoring systems, and network system. The most critical ones are electrical, mechanical and security system.

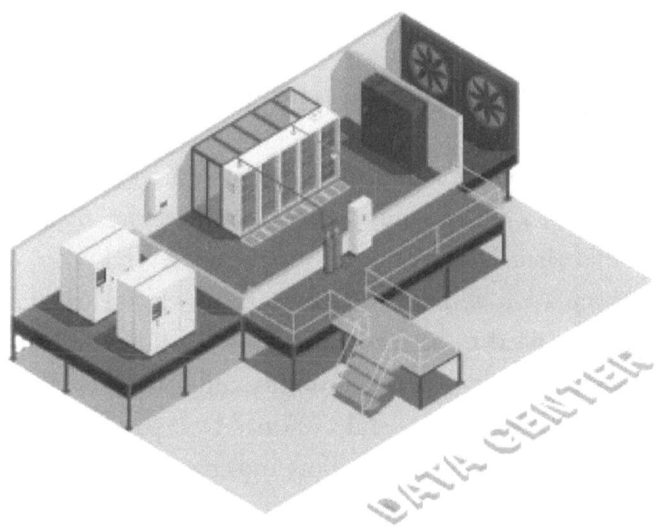

DATA CENTER

Datacentre Flexibility and Scalability

As discussed in chapter one, modern Datacentres should always be designed in a flexible and scalable way where the institution can guarantee that their Datacentre can survive for several years, without the need to replace it with a new Datacentre. Therefore, the following essential aspects need to be taken into consideration while designing the Datacentre, to guarantee the flexibility and scalability that ensures the ability to increase the size and workload by expanding the current infrastructure with the minimum effort and cost.

A. Site location

You have to choose the right location as per the requirements discussed in chapter one.

B. Building size

The size of the building should be larger than the current requirements as this allows you to expand the Datacentre in future with ease.

C. Floor layout

The layout of the Datacentre plays an essential role in future expansion, white space, network room, electricity room, uninterruptible power supply (UPS) room, standby diesel generator (DG) room and fire suppression room. It must be wide enough to accommodate additional equipment on future expansion.

D. Electrical system design

The electrical system needs a flexible (modular) design so that it can be expanded in future with ease. Therefore, the transformers, ring main units (RMUs), synchronization panels, DGs, Feeder pillar, distribution boards, remote power panel (RPP) and HV cables must be designed to be modular. It is recommended to initially install the required capacity and make a provision for future upgrades so that it can be comfortable and cost-effective to upgrade in future.

E. Mechanical design

One of the highly essential parts of the Datacentre design is the heating, ventilation, and air conditioning (HVAC) system. HVAC is the heart of the Datacentre. Therefore, it should be designed carefully to provide a perfect environment for critical equipment in the Datacentre. The future upgrade should be considered from the initial designing phase as this can guarantee that the future upgrade can be done with ease and cost-efficient.

F. Network Design

The network is one of the highly essential parts in the Datacentre design. Therefore, it must be designed in a way that it can provide the current and future required bandwidth and speed. And it must be in line with the latest available network implementation methodology. If a reasonable budget is available, then it is recommended to go for the latest smart network equipment.

———◉———

TIP : *One of the biggest challenges of the information systems specialist is the need for strenuous efforts to persuade administrators and financiers of the importance of the size and budget required for the Datacentre because they often think that it is a matter of exaggeration.*

Building Size and Floor Layout

A golden tip when you decide to build a Datacentre is to choose a suitable land area for future expansion and avoid being congested between other services. You also need to design the Datacentre wisely, and you need to study the size and weight of the equipment to be installed now and in the future to be able to decide the size of each section.

A suitable building design includes the following:

1. The location of white space

The white space room needs to be placed in the centre of the building so that the walls surrounding the room are not directly exposed to the outer space, and service rooms can surround it as a protection. The importance of this lies in reducing the external heat leakage or dust to the white space room directly and thus reducing the energy required to cool the Datacentre plus ensuring the cleanliness of the white space.

2. White space design

You need to design the size of each section in a way that it can accommodate the current required equipment along with the future expected equipment.

3. Internal heights of 5 metres

The recommended internal height (floor to ceiling) is 5 metres, and this is very important, especially if you are going to use a raised floor to support in-room cooling and false ceiling.

4. The height of the raised floor

The recommended height of the raised floor is 50cm to 80cm at least; this provides enough space for cold air to move smoothly.

5. White space area layout

To be able to determine the space required for the cabinets of servers, you need to know the number of cabinets currently required, the number of cabinets expected in the future, and the order of arrangements of the cabinets. Then layout a plan for space considering the appropriate spaces in front and behind the cabinets to allow free passage and airflow.

6. Office area, Network Operations Centre (NOC) and Security operations centre (SOC)

You need to have management offices for the admins and the Datacentre management along with NOC and SOC rooms, and you need to have the right space taking into account the type of equipment required in these rooms.

7. Conference/meeting rooms

Please note that you might need several meetings rooms with different capacities as Datacentre management requires a lot of internal and external meeting. Also, a conference room is highly required for Datacentre and needs to consider the space wisely as you won't want to come up with a conference or meeting room that can't accommodate your employees.

8. Communication room

This room can also be called Network room, and you need to have it with the correct size and at the correct location as close as possible to the white space. Communication room should be enough to accommodate the cabinets and other equipment such as computer room air conditioning (CRAC) units and fire suppression systems.

9. Equipment rooms

The equipment room is essential for Datacentre; it contains the power cabling, power protection, UPS, and distribution boards. Therefore, there should be two rooms for equipment for redundancy requirements and the size of these rooms must be enough for current and future requirements.

10. Battery room

Usually, there should be two battery rooms, which should be built near the equipment rooms. They must have proper ventilation, and the size should be sufficient to accommodate the batteries required for current and future requirements.

11. Stores

Stores are one of the essential rooms to be added to the design as it is much important; the Datacentre needs stores for the critical spare parts and consumable items.

12. Loading/unloading area and entrance

There should be back entrance and should be at least 2 metres wide; it is used for loading and unloading Datacentre heavy equipment. A loading ramp is also required.

13. Staging area

Some designers ignore the staging area, which is very important for testing the new equipment and making simulations before the final implementation on the live Datacentre. It is an essential part of the design and usually has an isolated network for simulation and testing.

14. Isolated Computer Room Air Conditioning (CRAC) units

The CRAC units need to be isolated than the white space to avoid service technicians from entering the white space for security reasons and to reduce the noise in the white space.

Electrical System Design

The electrical system is the most critical pillar of the Datacentre. Therefore, it should be appropriately designed, and the following are the major components of the electrical system:

Electrical Design

1. Standby Diesel Generator (DG)

THE DIESEL GENERATOR is an essential part of Datacentre; it provides electricity to Datacentre in case of primary grid failure. Therefore, it should be of a suitable size where the total load of the Datacentre must not exceed 80% of the total power of the generator.

2. Fuel tank (size and location)

The generator must be equipped with an internal diesel tank that can run for at least 8 hours and an external tank that can run for at least 36 hours. Commonly, at least 5000-litre tank is recommended. The external tank should be installed higher than the generator level to use the gravity to refill the generator's internal tank rather than using pumps that may subject to multiple problems.

3. Diesel filling control valve

This valve is installed to control the fuel filling process from the external tank to the generator's internal tank; it can be a solenoid valve or motorized valve.

4. Synchronization panel

Synchronization panel operates the process of running two or more DG sets in parallel on a shared line while matching the characteristics of each system as closely as possible. This is used in case of the inability of a single generator to supply the power required for the total load of the Datacentre. Here, the synchronization panel runs two or more generators at the same time when required to provide the necessary load for the Datacentre.

5. Automatic Transfer Switch (ATS)

ATS is a panel that detects when the mains electricity supply fails and trigger the standby generator control panel to start the generator to provide the necessary power to the Datacentre.

6. Uninterruptible Power Supply (UPS)

UPS is a device that stores electrical power on batteries. When the mainline goes off, it provides the critical load in the Datacentre with the necessary power. This process allows the servers and other sensitive equipment to continue running until the standby generator takes over the load. It automatically transfers the load from the battery to the mainline.

7. Electrical distribution (dual paths)

The Datacentre should have two different electricity paths to guarantee a real redundancy. So, the high voltage (HV) and low voltage (LV) cables need to be routed through separate paths starting from the grid to transformers, from transformers to the main distribution room, from the main distribution room to the Datacentre electricity room and finally to the active components cabinets.

8. Building feeds, conduits, and trenches

The building feeds must be designed by an electrical engineer who has experience with Datacentres or works with Datacentres consultant. When designing conduits and trenches, security, safety and future expansion must be considered. For example, if the cooling units required now are 6 and you expect the units to be 15 in future, then the conduits and trenches should be made wider enough to accommodate the 15 units piping and cables.

9. Remote Power Panel (RPP)

RPP, also called Floor Mount Power Distribution Unit (FMPDU), is meant to provide the cabinets with power. RPP/FMPDU is installed as two sets, and each set is connected to an independent electricity power line. Each server cabinet is connected to both independent RPP/FMPDU sets for redundancy purposes. These units have a limited number of power connectors; therefore, we have to choose the correct size that can support the current requirement and can be easily upgraded to support future requirements.

It is recommended to go for busbar system instead of using cables and RPP/FMPDU as it supports future expansion with ease (*busbar system will be discussed in detail in Chapter 6*).

10. Power strips/Power Distribution Units (PDUs)

Each server cabinet usually has two PDUs or power strips and each is connected to independent RPP or separate busbar line as this is very important for redundancy. PDUs comes in several types; it can be dummy, monitored or switched (*power strips will be discussed in detail in Chapter 6*).

TIP : *The electrical system must be given utmost importance and must be planned by an electrical engineer specialised in Datacentres to avoid unpleasant surprises.*

Mechanical Design

Mechanical systems are the second most crucial Datacentre pillar, and they consume massive electrical power much more than any other system in the Datacentre. So, they must be designed carefully by a specialist to guarantee the efficacy of the Datacentre and can be generally summarised as follows:

1. Heating, ventilation, and air conditioning (HVAC) system

This system can either be direct expansion (DX) cooling or chilled water cooling system (Schiller) type. The chilled water cooling system (Schiller) type is more expansive and complicated, but its efficiency is higher than DX cooling. Typically, DX cooling is used for small Datacentres while large Datacentres require Schiller type.

In Schiller system, the water is chilled in the schillers outside the Datacentre and then pumped into the evaporators inside, where the blowers blow the air through the evaporators to extract the heat from the Datacentre, take it out via water, and the water returns to the chiller again.

Schiller system

BUT IN DX COOLING, the refrigerant gas compressed to huge condensers outside the building. These condensers are equipped with fans that blow air into them to get rid of heat carried out by refrigerant gas. The gas is compressed into an evaporator inside the Datacentre which is also equipped with powerful fans that blow air from the Datacentre through it. The evaporator sucks the heat and takes it outside the Datacentre.

DX cooling

2. Capacity

THE REQUIRED COOLING capacity should be calculated accurately by an expert based on the required temperature inside the Datacentre that suites the type of equipment to install. After the calculation process, it is necessary to add a safety percentage to ensure effectiveness (*this calculation will be discussed in detail in Chapter 7 - DC Electricity/Cooling Load calculation*).

3. Distribution

Air distribution is essential for sufficient cooling. Therefore, we must have a mechanism where its possible to add extra air vent, reduce or increase airflow. With in-room cooling, we can accomplish this by using adjustable perforated raised floor tiles.

4. Cooling and heating

This system provides cooling for the Datacentre where the hot air generated through the cooling process can be used to heat the offices in cold countries, and this adds more efficiency to the system and saves money.

5. Humidity control

One of the most critical systems in the Datacentre is the humidifier. It is a system that controls the level of humidity in the Datacentre to be on an acceptable level. This can be accomplished by generating humidity if the humidity level is less than the recommended level, or extract humidity, convert it to water and drain it outside the Datacentre if the humidity is higher than the required level.

6. Ventilation system

This system is used to keep the Datacentre air fresh. A sensor measures the internal air quality to decide when it is essential to add some fresh air into the Datacentre atmosphere. The system can be configured to start this process when the outside temperature is near the internal temperature to avoid affecting the internal temperature severely. The air is filtered before it comes inside the Datacentre.

7. Air Filtering

The air inside the Datacentre is continuously filtered to keep the Datacentre clean. The suitable CRAC unit filters are generally compatible with particulate levels coarse (2.5–15 μm and fine 0.1–2.5 μm).

TIP : *The Datacentre cooling system should be given exceptional importance because it is the second most crucial element in the structure of the Datacentre and may cause significant disasters if poorly designed.*

Fire Suppression System

1. Very Early Smoke Detection Apparatus (VESDA)

VESDA is a system that analyses the air particles inside the Datacentre continuously. If there is any disturbance in the air, this means that there is a possibility of smoke leading to a fire at any moment and to avoid this, the alarm system fires off and identifies the suspected area; therefore, it is an essential anticipatory system to detect fires early.

2. Smoke detection

This system uses heat/smoke detection to discover the fire in the Datacentre and then sends a signal to the fire suppression system to work. In case of mistake, it gives the DC admins some seconds to switch it off before triggering the fire suppression system.

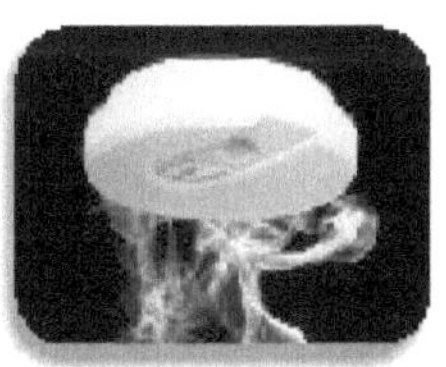

Smoke sensor

3. Gas fire suppression system

IT IS A SYSTEM THAT uses a specific gas to extinguish the fire. Usually, the gas neutralises the oxygen gas that helps ignite the flame. Even though the gas is not safe for people, it is safe for the equipment and doesn't cause any damages. There are several types such as halon, FM200 and Novec 1230.

4. Pre-action wet systems

A pre-action system is a hybrid system for dry/wet fire protection where the tubes are filled with compressed air, the spray heads are all closed, and the water is isolated from the tubes by a control valve.

When the system is triggered, the air comes out from the spray where the fire starts and the fire gets extinguished. Although this system is safe for human, it destroys the equipment.

5. Oxygen Reduction Fire Prevention System

It is a system that prevents the development or spreading of fire by adding nitrogen to the atmosphere. This is done by reducing the oxygen to a level that it doesn't allow the fire to ignite at all. Although the low oxygen level may cause respiratory stress on workers inside the Datacentre, it can be increased for extended periods when the technicians are present. The maintenance of this system is costly.

TIP : *Using Pre-action wet systems to control fire in Datacentre is a significant risk unless there is a redundant active Datacentre connected to the primary one. The water extinguishing might eradicate the devices and requires cutting off the electrical current entirely from the Datacentre. Therefore, using the oxygen control systems or gas systems is safer on the devices.*

Security System

1. Closed-circuit television (CCTV)

CCTV monitoring is an essential part of the Datacentre. Every person coming to the Datacentre needs to be monitored, including the external fence, the main gate, the transformers, the generators, and all of the interior rooms. The recording server must be equipped with failover technology. It must keep the records for at least 60 days. The quality and the resolution must be high enough to identify any face or car plate number. For indoor cameras, the CCTVs should be equipped by 20 metres Infrared light (IR) for night vision and 60 to 100 metres IR for outdoor cameras.

Camera types

2. Access control

THE ACCESS CONTROL system is a physical security system that controls who can access the system, including when and how. It is vital to choose a robust system that can offer the security admin the right tools to manage the employee's authentication and authorisation.

The main white space and electricity and cooling systems doors must be protected with a fingerprint readers (FP) control system with at least dual authentication such as fingerprint and card.

The main Datacentre door should be equipped with a double reader for entrance and exit to monitor the employee access and exit time.

Always choose an access control system that supports the authentication via active directory because it adds extra flexibility for the management.

Card reader

3. Centralised monitoring

ACCESS CONTROL CENTRALISED monitoring is critical because the security officer needs to have a clear and live view of physical security. It helps to identify any security breach warning immediately on the screen. The security system should always be integrated with CCTV so that the security officer can visually monitor any breach either immediately or later.

4. The automated gates and barriers

The main gates must be connected to the access control system, and it should be equipped with Hydraulic Rising Traffic Bollards to avoid car crash attacks, and guards must always be available by the gate.

———◦———

TIP : *Special care is essential when choosing an access control system. It should support the link to the fire control system and can be linked to the active directory so that it is easy to add authenticated users and the right authorisation.*

Chapter 3: Internal Building Requirements

Interior design of the Datacentre

The interior design of the Datacentre is very important and neglecting it may lead to very complex future problems. Therefore, it is always recommended to entrust the design to a professional specialising in Datacentres as he/she knows the needs of buildings and can anticipate the future and design in an easy way for future expansion.

Datacentre Floor

Datacentre floor has so many specifications that need to be considered. This is because the weight of today's cabinets and equipment cabinets can cause stress on the floor structures, making it crucial to consider floor-loading requirements in your Datacentre design.

———◉———

CABINETS TODAY CAN handle 1000-1400kg, which is a significant load on the floor other than UPS and the weight of battery cabinets. Therefore, you have to consider the following essential points while designing the floor, especially if your white space and equipment rooms are on a floor higher than the ground floor.

———◉———

KNOWING THE PLANNED type of the server cabinets is essential to figure out the total load to be on the floor and the required strength of the columns on the floor. As per the recommended specifications, you can follow the below guidelines:

———◉———

FOR CABINETS WITH FOOTPRINT 6 Sq.ft and weigh not more than 454kg, the average floor loading should be 83 pounds (lbs) per square foot (PSF) (38kg PSF).

———◉———

FOR CABINETS WITH FOOTPRINT 7 Sq.ft and weigh not more than 454kg, the average floor loading should be 67 pounds (lbs) per square foot (PSF) (31kg PSF).

———●———

FOR CABINETS WITH FOOTPRINT 8.8 Sq.ft and weigh not more than 454kg, the average floor loading should be 67 pounds (lbs) per square foot (PSF) (24kg PSF).

TIP : *Never use a higher floor in any building as a Datacentre unless it is initially designed for this purpose. Otherwise, you will encounter dangerous cracks that may cause the floor to collapse due to the heaviness of the server racks.*

Datacentre Floor Coatings

The Datacentre floor must be coated with special Epoxy coat, especially the floor under the raised floor. Epoxy coating is a coating compound that consists of two elements (epoxy resin and a polyamine hardener).

Epoxy coating

THE ADVANTAGES OF EPOXY flooring for Datacentres are as follows:

- **Prevention of water leak effects**

In case of any water leak, the Epoxy layer prevents the floor and walls from the effect of water.

- **Crack resistance**

Its semi-flexible surface allows it to resist cracks even if heavy items dropped on its surface.

- **Dust prevention**

It eliminates the natural dust produced by untreated concrete that can affect the air cooling units and the servers.

- **Anti-Slip surface**

Epoxy is flexible in nature and thus prevents slipping and maintains general safety.

- **Better decoration and easy to clean**

The epoxy has a very nice look that adds a bright touch to the floor.

Raised Floor

The raised floor is used in the Datacentre for several reasons, such as to route power and network cables under the Datacentre and to give better decoration to the Datacentre. It is also used as a lower passage for the Datacentre air cooling.

Raised floor

THE MODERN DATACENTRE can be designed without a raised floor in the case of using in-row or in-cabinet cooling system, where the power and network cables come from the top. The raised floor is preferred for large Datacentres as cooling usually comes from down while the power and data cables come from the top. It is always recommended to use anti-static raised floor tiles that can be connected to a particular earthling system to get rid of any static electricity.

The recommended height of the raised floor is 50 to 80cm from the ground. It should be fire-rated and should be able to hold the expected server cabinets load.

For standard access floors, panel load ratings usually range from 1,000-2,500 pounds (455–1134kg), allowing for more reliable floors that can support heavy, bulky equipment and can be measured as follows:

Required Duty	Required ultimate load	
	kilo Newton(KN)	Kilo Gram
Light Duty	8.8 KN	897.35 KG
Medium Duty	11.25 KN	1147.18 KG
Heavy Duty	14.50 KN	1478.59 KG
Extra Heavy Duty	18.36 KN	1872.2 KG

False Ceiling

The existence of a false ceiling is not necessary for all Datacentres. While some designers prefer not to use the false ceiling to keep the top area open for the ease of maintenance, others insist on using it.

False Ceiling

FALSE CEILING HAS SOME advantages that can be summarised as follows:

◈ Reduces the space of cold aisle area that requires cooling. If you use cold aisle containment, then you can reduce the amount of space of the cold aisle (*a cold-aisle containment separates the hot and cold airstreams for extreme efficiency*). If you use hot aisle containment, then you might reduce the amount of space at the hot aisle, and both can lead to better cooling efficiency.

◇ Can enhance control of ducted air in the hot/cold aisle containment. That is, it can be used to hide the cooling air duct.

◇ Helps to maintain cleanliness inside the Datacentre. It makes the inside of the Datacentre looks clean and provides a better look for the inside area.

◇ Lighting, occupancy sensors, and fire sensors fixed to the false ceiling.

TIP : *Since the Datacentre is not a human comfort zone, it is best to avoid using the false ceiling for a clean and more straightforward maintenance.*

Fire-Rated Doors

Fire-rated doors are highly required in the Datacentre building. This is to reduce the spread of fire inside the Datacentre and also seal the internal area to guarantee the fire suppression system efficiency.

Fire-rated door

THE FOLLOWING NEEDS to be noted and considered when choosing the Datacentre doors:

◇ Metal fire doors can attain ratings up to 3 hours while wood fire doors can be rated for about 90 minutes.

◇ The external doors are recommended to be a steel fire rated doors with above 180 minutes rating.

◇ The internal doors can be wooden fire-rated doors with 90 minutes rating.

⬦ All fire emergency doors must either be equipped with push bar or access control device controlled by the fire panel.

⬦ Doors need to be entirely sealed to prevent the suppression system gas leakage outside the room in case of fire.

Windows

Windows are not preferred in Datacentre, especially for the white space, due to a number of disadvantages listed below:

Window protection with metal grid

◇ Windows can leak heat into the Datacentre, which can severely affect the cooling efficiency and cause more indirect expenses on the required electrical power.

◇ Windows can leak dust into the Datacentre, which can cause several issues in the cooling system and the servers, as it blocks the cooling filters in no time.

◇ It is not safe in the event of a fire. Windows can leak fire extinguishing gas outside the protected area, which leads to a lower gas concentration that might cause low effectiveness of the fire suppression system.

◇ Due to the safety and security requirements, you have to protect windows by a metal grid if you cannot avoid it.

Loading/Unloading Ramp

Datacentre ramp is highly required by the Datacentre since the technicians usually handle heavy equipment that requires a suitable ramp. The slope is ideally needed to be 6 feet (1.8 meters) wide and should have landings at both ends (1.8 square meters).

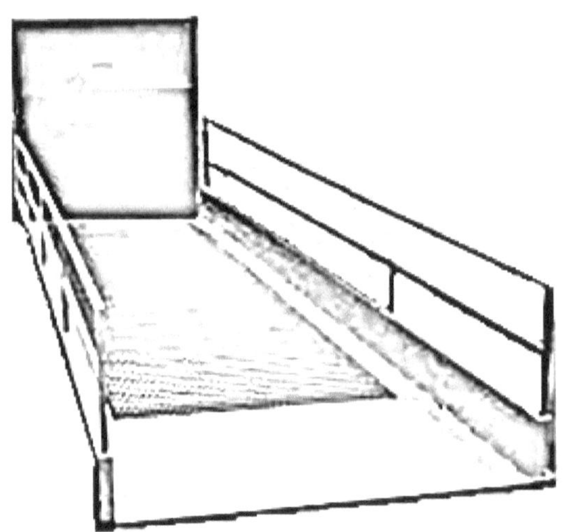

Datacentre Server Lift

S erver lift makes the Datacentre server handling easy and can be used by anyone to transport, position, install or remove any cabinet or server in Datacentre safely and accurately with minimal effort.

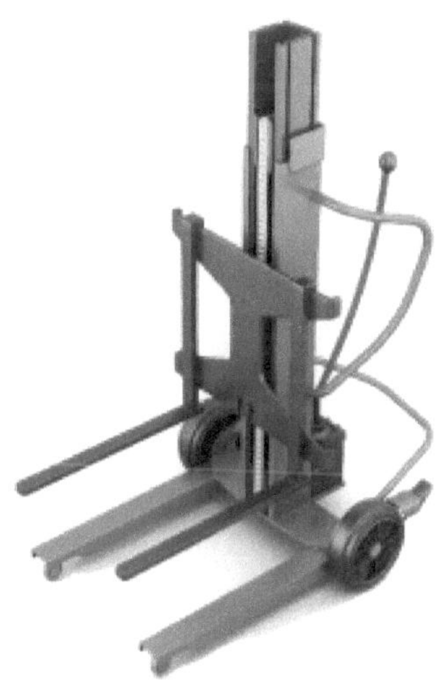

Server Lift

Chapter 4: HVAC and Ventilation System

Heating, Ventilation, and Air Conditioning

Heating, Ventilation, and Air Conditioning (HVAC) is the system responsible for controlling the temperature and humidity in the Datacentre. It is configured to keep the optimal ambient temperature range in the Datacentre, which is usually between 70-74°F (20-24°C) and the relative humidity (RH) to be between 40%-60%. The temperature range is based on the type of active components used in the Datacentre, and the new servers can run on higher temperature compared with the old servers.

THE TYPICAL COOLING systems are direct expansion (DX) cooling and chilled water cooling. The designer decides the most suitable system for the Datacentre based on the size of the Datacentre and the available space and cost. It is worth mentioning that chilled water cooling requires large independent areas for water chillers.

THE HUMIDIFIER IS AN essential part of the cooling systems because it helps to control the level of humidity in the Datacentre. Also, using an effective system for monitoring the temperature and humidity is highly required.

Chilled Water Cooling System

Chilled water systems include HVAC equipment designed to exchange heat for services such as computer room. The chilled water absorbs the heat from the building using chilled water. It then returns it to the chiller to remove the heat from the water using the refrigeration process.

Chiller cooling

Direct Expansion (DX) Cooling System

A direct expansion air conditioning (DX) unit cools indoor air using condensed refrigerant gas. The refrigerant absorbs the heat from the building and then return it to the outdoor condenser where the condenser removes the heat from the refrigerant using the heat exchange process.

DX cooling

Humidifiers/Dehumidifiers

To control the ambient relative humidity levels, we need a humidifier. Humidifiers are used to add the needed water vapour back into the cooling equipment air stream. Dehumidifiers, however, are used to reduce humidity by collecting extra humidity as water and then drip it into a drainage pipe outside the Datacentre.

HUMIDIFIERS MIGHT BE inbuilt in the cooling system or can come as a standalone device. The majority of the Datacentre cooling system comes with an in-built humidifier for better performance and integrity.

Importance of Humidifiers

A. It keeps the relative humidity (RH) in server rooms and Datacentres between 40%-60%, or as per the technicians setting.

B. It prevents moisture on motherboards, hard drives, and in connecting sockets to avoid quick damage, corrosion and equipment failure.

C. It prevents the atmosphere from getting too dry, which might result in the buildup of static electricity on the systems that might cause damages.

Humidifiers Water Inlet and Drainage

Humidifier needs to be connected to a water source to be able to generate humidity when required, and this process needs some precautions because the existence of water source inside the Datacentre is risky. But since there is no other option, it is essential to consider the following:

A. Good pipe quality

It is imperative to use quality water pipes to prevent the risk of water leakage.

B. Blockage risk

The drain pipe is subject to blockage since it might cause leakage inside the Datacentre. Consequently, the drainage tube should be protected with proper netting to avoid rats and other harmful insects; it also requires continuous maintenance.

C. Monitoring the leakage

The supply pipes need to be monitored by the water leakage alarm system to discover any leakage immediately.

D. Dangerous flashback

The drainage can cause a flashback of water to the Datacentre. Therefore, it needs to be routed to separate drainage line other than other services drainage line.

HVAC Redundancy
79

HVAC is a critical system for the Datacentre because the Datacentre cannot run without cooling. Thus, we have to provide the Datacentre with a redundant cooling system. This means in case of failure of a set of units, another set takes over the cooling load. We have several designs for redundancy, where "N" represents the exact amount of devices needed, and the extra devices represent +1.

N redundancy

This method is simply the capacity required to cool Datacentre. It represents the cooling power you need for the servers. There is no redundancy, so the failure of the cooling system means that the whole cooling stops.

N+1 redundancy

This method contains redundant equipment and runs on common circuitry. So, if two cooling units are available, add a third extra unit, and in case of a failure of any of the two primary units, the third takes its place.

2N redundancy

This method doubles the amount of equipment needed, which run separately with no single points of failure. In this scenario, if the Datacentre needs two cooling units, then another two units will be added. This can take the whole cooling load in case of failure of the primary unit.

2N+1 redundancy

This method is doubling the amount needed and adding an extra piece of equipment. In this scenario, if the Datacentre needs two cooling units, then another two units will be added to take the whole cooling load in case of failure of the primary unit. Further, another extra unit is added to take over the role of any single unit failure.

Availability Model

Two cooling sets one active
and another standby,
Plus one extra unit.

Important Notice

It is essential to use all of the cooling units at the same level of wear and tear to avoid reaching the end of life of the main units where the standby units are still unused. This can be achieved by using the standby unit from time to time (at least every 24 hours) to take over the load of one of the main units. Doing this keeps it active and ensure it is ready to be used when needed. This process can be automated without human intervention.

Temperature and Humidity Sensors

As discussed earlier, the optimal temperature range for the Datacentre is between 20 to 24 °C. ASHRAE also recommended 65°F to 80°F, 18°C to 27°C temperature range. This range is directly related to the type of existing equipment installed in the Datacentre.

YOU NEED TO MONITOR these levels closely; humidity and temperature sensors can be placed inside the IT equipment cabinet to monitor temperature and humidity. It is crucial to monitor all of the servers because usually, the lower sensor reads lower temperatures while you need to know the correct temperature of all of the cabinet servers to ensure that they are within the recommended range. Therefore, sensors should be placed at the bottom, middle and top of the front side of the rack.

TIP : *New servers can generally operate at temperatures above the average rate, as this leads to a saving in electrical energy used for cooling. So, be aware of the optimal temperature recommended by the manufacturer of the servers and adjust the cooling systems as required.*

Free Cooling System and Ventilation

Free cooling is the use of the outside temperature to cool the Datacentre. Free cooling can only be used in cold places where the external temperature is less than the required internal temperature; this helps to reduce the cooling cost of the Datacentre.

***

USING THE FREE COOLING technology can also enhance the Datacentre air quality, by bringing fresh air inside the Datacentre, but this requires proper filtering for the incoming air.

Cooling Types

The Datacentre cooling methods have gone through several enhancements targeting the point where the best cooling method can be achieved along with cost-efficiency.

Traditional In-room Cooling

The In-room cooling type is simply a traditional way of cooling Datacentres.

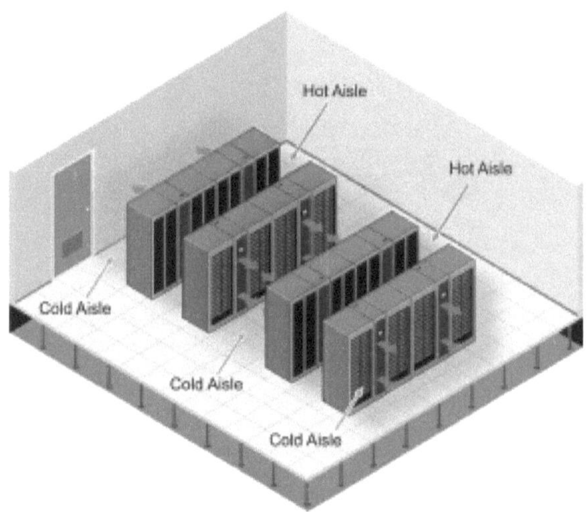

Traditional in-room cooling

TRADITIONAL COOLING Drawbacks

Since this cooling system cools the whole room and not only targeting the server's inlet, then one of its disadvantages is that it requires high cooling power which is costly.

Also, since there is no isolation between the cold and hot air, they both get mixed, then comes out of the servers and return to the servers as warm air. This drawback severely affects the cooling efficiency.

ANOTHER DRAWBACK IS that this cooling method has several hot spots in the Datacentre due to the unequal cooling points and bad cooling distribution.

Cold/Hot Aisle Containment Cooling

One of the improved cooling methods is Cold/Hot aisle containment cooling and is a modern way of cooling Datacentres.

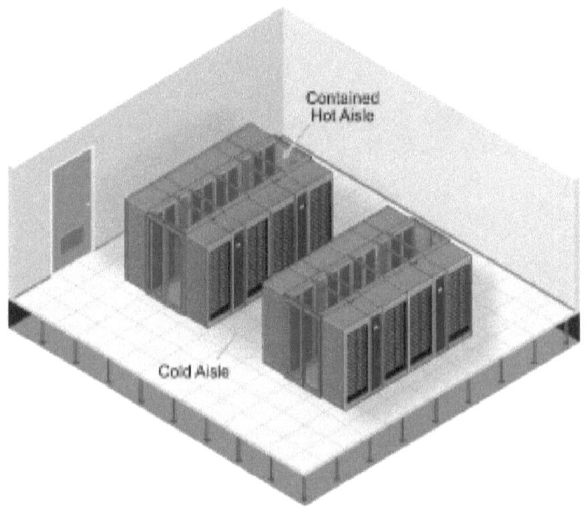

Hot aisle containment cooling

ADVANTAGES OF CONTAINMENT Cooling

It requires less power. This is very important as it helps to reach good Power Usage Effectiveness (PUE) level.

Air wholly isolated. The cold air is completely isolated from the hot air, which increases the cooling efficiency by minimising the amount of cold air required to cool the servers.

AVOID HOT SPOTS. IT becomes easy to increase the airflow in front of some cabinets and reduce for others based on requirements, and this avoids the hot spots.

EQUAL COOLING POINTS. The cold air can be controlled in each zone, where it is easy to control the flow of air in each zone separately.

In-row Cooling

In-row cooling precisely cools the air closest to the server cabinets. It is installed beside the server cabinets in the Hot/Cold aisle area, and the width of the cooling unit can either be 30cm or 60cm.

In-row cooling

THIS COOLING METHOD is similar to the Hot/Cold Aisle cooling. The only difference is that here, the cooling device is beside the server cabinet, and it does not require a raised floor.

In-cabinet Cooling

In-cabinet cooling system cools down the servers placed within a closed cabinet. This system is best for a small number of cabinets such as one or two cabinets, while some designers used it for more number of cabinets.

In-cabinet cooling

IN-CABINET COOLING has the following advantages:

1. Real-time information and supervision at cabinet-level.

2. Fast response capability and regulation of the cooling unit operation.

3. The airflow is entirely contained within the cabinet.

4. Air conditioning is independent of the room conditions (heat and dust).

5. Can be implemented in rooms not configured as a Datacentre.

6. Can be implemented in rooms whose initial layout is not intended for high-density needs.

7. Requires little space.

8. Thermally neutral with the room.

TIP : *Through professional experience, I found out that the Cold/Hot aisle containment cooling method is the most effective way to cool medium to large Datacentres, provided that they are properly planned.*

Computer Room Air Conditioning Isolation

In the Datacentre cold/hot aisle method, it is always recommended to isolate the computer room air conditioning (CRAC) from the white space. This is very important to avoid the existence of cooling system technicians inside the Datacentre white space, and it helps in cooling efficacy and security purpose.

CRAC unit

Use a separate Unit for each purpose

1. The primary Datacentre cooling must be isolated from the other rooms, such as Network, electricity and battery rooms. This is very important due to the following:

2. Variation in required cooling temperature. Each system has different temperature and humidity requirements.

3. Fire separation system. Each room has a separate separation system, so it must be isolated from other rooms.

4. The criticality of the room. Not all of the rooms need continuous cooling; for example, the electricity room can run for hours without cooling while the white space cannot.

5. Redundancy requirements. Not all of the rooms require a full redundancy mainly if N+N is used.

Cooling Units Power Redundancy

Now that we have discussed the redundancy of the cooling devices, what about the redundancy of electricity feed for each cooling unit? The cooling units typically do not have inbuilt dual power supply like the servers. Therefore, we need a device that can connect the cooling unit to the live power source and automatically transfer it to the second source once the first source is interrupted.

THE STATIC TRANSFER switch (STS) can perform this task. So, STS is automatic switching equipment designed to transfer electric loads between two independent AC power sources without interruption.

Chapter 5: Safety Systems

Very Early Smoke Detection Apparatus System

VESDA system is crucial to discover the fire in the Datacentre as early as possible, and this is easily achievable by using the latest technology. One of the technologies available in the market is the VESDA detector, which is much like a vacuum cleaner. It works by continuously absorbing air from the protected environment through dedicated purpose inhaled tubes and fittings, which tests the air quality that passes through the VESDA laser room for detection. If it detects any abnormal components in the air, it raises an alert and can stimulate the fire system automatically as a proactive measure to control the fire.

VESDA-E VEA Addressable Aspirating Smoke Detector

VEA combines VESDA reliability and early warning smoke detection along with pinpoint addressability. VEA uses patented multi-channel microbore tubes and patented air-sampling points with three sensitivity settings. Using this technology make the identification of the exact location of the risk much accurate and specific. This is highly essential to find out whether there is a real risk or fake alarm because even thick dust can trigger an alarm.

Fire Detection and Suppression System

Automatic fire detection and suppression system control and extinguish fires without human intervention. Examples of automatic systems include a fire sprinkler system, gaseous fire suppression, and condensed aerosol fire suppression.

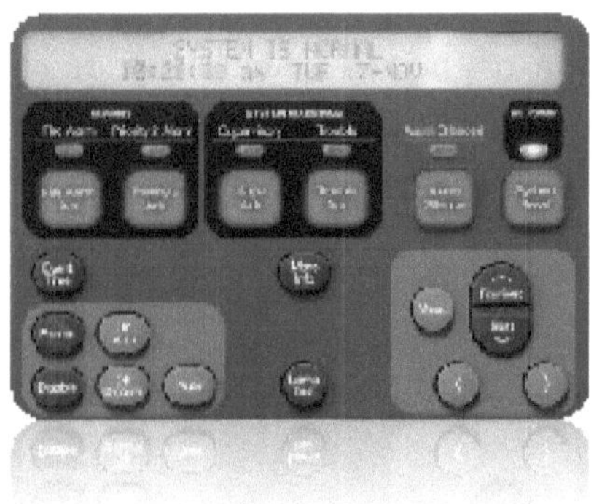

Fire control panel

THE FOLLOWING ARE THE most used fire extinguishing systems:

- **Halon**: a liquefied compressed gas clean agent that stops the spread of fire by chemically disrupting combustion. It is electrically non-conducting. In 1989, the Montreal Protocol determined halon as one of the reasons depleting the ozone layer; therefore, it has been banned and no longer used.

- **FM-200**: a clean agent fire suppression system. Although the Datacentre designers move to an ozone-friendly fire suppression system, FM-200 is still the most widely used fire suppression gas in Datacentre.

• **Northern Virginia Electric Cooperative (Novec 1230)**: a clean agent fire suppression and fire extinguishing system that removes thermal elements or free radicals from the fire triangle. This agent does not remove oxygen, so it is safer on a human being than FM-200 and is ozone friendly.

• **Oxygen reduction fire prevention system**: It is also known as Hypoxic air technology for fire prevention. It prevents the development or spreading of fire by adding nitrogen to the air inside the Datacentre. This system intends to reduce the oxygen level below 15% by displacing it with argon/nitrogen. It also takes into consideration the safety of server room personnel by keeping oxygen levels above 12% to protect anyone present. Low oxygen level may cause respiratory stress on workers inside the Datacentre. So, it may require increases in the level of oxygen when the technicians are present inside the Datacentre for long periods. It is also worth mentioning that the costs of maintaining this system may be higher than other systems.

• **Dry pipe water extinguishing system**: This system uses sprinklers attached to a piping system containing compressed air. A central control valve opens and releases water to the sprinklers in case of fire. Although this system can cause damages on the servers since it uses water, it is very safe for humans and is usually used in a Datacentre that has another replica active Datacentre.

Gas Nozzles and Fire Detectors Locations

The fire detectors and gas nozzles must be located in the correct location to maintain the best possible efficiency of the fire separation system. Therefore, the following should be considered when designing the fire suppression system:

AS A RULE, SMOKE DETECTORS can cover a radius of six meters, and the maximum distance between two smoke alarms should be nine meters. This is in compliance with the National Fire Protection Association (NFPA). The nozzles and detectors should be installed in the following locations:

- Above the false ceiling.
- Inside the room.
- Below the raised floor.

Cold/hot aisle containment can either be equipped with an auto-open roof or a gas nozzle installed inside the cold/hot aisle containment.

Other Fire Suppression Requirements

The automatic suppression system is required to be installed separately in the following rooms in the Datacentre:

1. White space.
2. Network room.
3. Battery room.
4. Electricity/UPS room.

It is recommended to use both heat and smoke detection system to discover the fire as early as possible. Portable fire extinguishers should be installed in place. The central fire system must be equipped with manual pull stations, and finally, it is crucial to adhere to National Fire Protection Association (NFPA) Standard on Automatic Fire Detectors (72E) while designing the fire system.

How to Calculate the Required Gas Capacity

The calculation for the required amount of gas for each room is necessary. Each gas has its calculation method based on the gas concentration level. For example, FM200 has a concentration level between 6% and 9% while Novec 1230 has a concentration level between 4% and 6%. Please note that the amount of agent to be used for Novec 1230 is more than FM200.

FM200 IS CHOSEN AS an example for our calculation, so to calculate the required amount of FM200 for the Datacentre, it is essential to follow the below steps:

1. Know the fire class you use as a base for the calculation:

• **Class A Fire**: Fire in ordinary combustible materials, such as wood, cloth, paper, rubber, and plastics.

• **Class B Fire**: Fire in inflammable liquids, oils, greases, tars, oil-based paints, lacquers, and flammable gases.

- **Class C Fire**: Fire that involves energised electrical equipment where the electrical resistivity of the extinguishing media is of importance.

For Datacentre, we consider fire class C.

2. Find the room area, for example, a room size Length 50 ft X Width 32 ft X Height 16 ft =25,600.

◈ **W = Weight of FM200 (lb)**

◈ **V = Net Volume of the Hazard (25600 ft³)**

◈ **C = FM 200 Design Concentration (7%)**

◈ **Sf = Safety factor (1.2)**

◈ **RC = Resulting Concentration = C*sf (8.4%)**

◈ **t = Minimum anticipated temperature of the protected volume. (70F)**

◈ **S = Specific Volume of superheated agent vapour at 1 atmosphere and the temperature t. (2.2075 ft³/lb)**

$$\text{Step 1: } W = \frac{V}{S}\left[\frac{RC}{1000-RC}\right]$$

$$\text{Step 2: } W = \frac{V25600}{2.2075}\left[\frac{8.4}{100-8.4}\right]$$

Step 3: W= 1064 lbs of FM200 agent

Result : W= 482.62kg

Note: The calculations listed above are indicative only and may vary from standard to others.

Fire Control and Precautions

◇ Use fire stopper whenever applicable. In the case of routing cables to other rooms, it is highly essential to use a particular fire stopper.

◇ Make sure the doors are appropriately sealed to stop fire spread and gas leakage.

◇ Keep the doors shut and monitor it. The doors should be monitored by access control to guarantee that they are always shut and opened for seconds only.

◇ Don't store any flammable items in the Datacentre, such as boxes, flammable fluids, and furniture.

Water Leakage Detection System

One of the Datacentre's worst enemies is water, so there should be a mechanism to detect water leakage in the Datacentre, and as long as the water is heavy, it should be detected at the floor level. Therefore, the detection system is installed under the raised floor. It is always recommended to route the detection cable below the cooling system water lines, especially for the chilled water system.

Rodent Repellent System

Another thing that Datacentres suffer from is the entry of rats, which pose a real danger as they strongly tend to bite wires such as data cables and electrical wires. This may ultimately lead to the disruption of the Datacentre. Therefore, an effective method called rodent repellent system should be used to prevent rats from entering the Datacentre. This is an intelligent system that helps in keeping the rodent away from the protected area by generating high-frequency ultrasonic sounds.

Chapter 6: Datacentre Electrical Systems

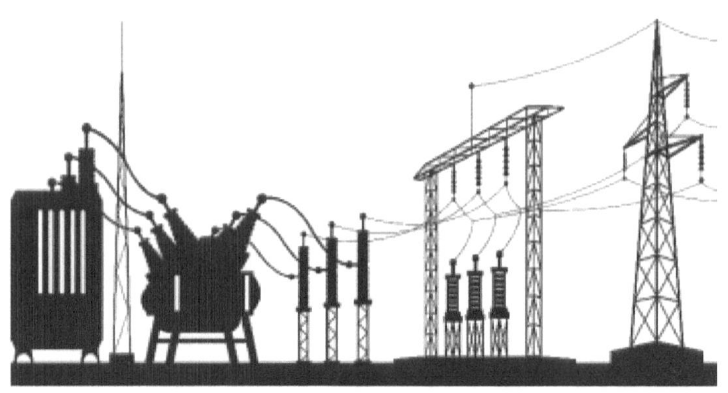

Electrical System Planning

The electrical system is the heartbeat of the Datacentre, and it is the most expensive system in the Datacentre. It is also the most budget consuming system since it is one of the Datacentre pillars. The electrical system is the main part that determines the Tier of the Datacentre, as explained in Chapter 1. This tiering is mainly determined based on the way the electrical system is designed, and must therefore be given utmost importance.

The layout of the electrical system is the most critical part as it needs special attention and tremendous efforts, and the periodic testing of this system is essential to ensure that it works as intended. Therefore, it is considered an essential part of the Disaster Recovery Plan (DRP).

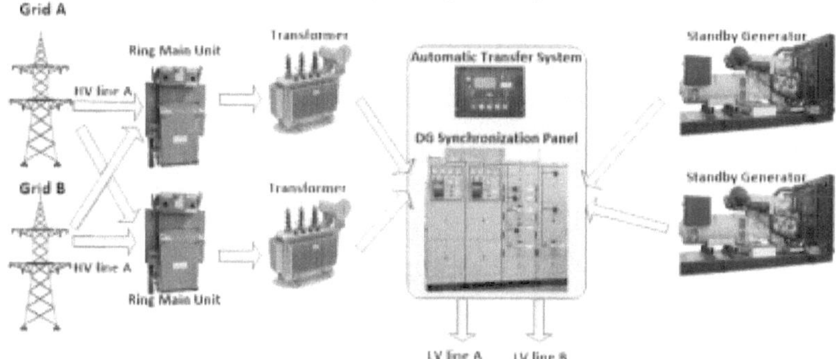

THE ABOVE IMAGE DESCRIBES an optimal design for the outer part of the Datacentre electrical system for Tier 4 Datacentre; it contains the essential components of the system, namely grid lines, RMUs, Transformers, Synchronisation panel, ATS and generator.

TIP : *Attention must be paid to the design of the electrical system to avoid future problems that could lead to the collapse of the Datacentre.*

Ring Main Unit (RMU)

RMU is a standard piece of switchgear installed in distribution systems comprising switches for switching power cable rings and switches in series with fuses for the protection of distribution transformers. This switch is used to manually transfer the load from one grid to another in case of any failure.

Ring Main Unit (RMU)

Transformer

Transformer is an electrical device that converts alternating current from one voltage to another. Transformer is basically of two types, a "step up" or "step down." In the Datacentre electric system, step down is typically used since it converts High Voltage (HV) to Low Voltage (LV) so that it can be used to run Datacentre electrical appliances.

Transformer

Feeder Pillar

A feeder pillar is also called a power box in the USA. It is a cabinet for electrical equipment, controlling the electrical supply to several services. It is typically installed close to the transformer and have LV power. Feeder pillar provides a simple way for cables connection and ease of maintenance.

Feeder pillar

Standby Generator

A standby generator is essential for the Datacentre and is designed to provide the Datacentre with the necessary electrical power in case any failure occurred with the primary electricity grid. There should be at least one standby generator in the Datacentre.

THE STANDBY GENERATOR capacity must be 125% of the Datacentre load. For example, if the total load of the Datacentre is 100KVA, then the standby generator capacity should be at least 125KVA. This is very important to avoid any interruption if there is a sudden increase of load on the generator.

IT IS CRUCIAL TO KEEP the generator warm during the standby status, and it should always be above 40°F/4.5°C. Therefore, if the Datacentre is located in a cold area, a heater needs to be installed inside the generator room to keep it warm so that it can start easily and faster when required.

THE STANDBY GENERATOR needs to be equipped with at least 8 hours internal diesel tank. This is to guarantee that the generator can run for enough time without the need to be refilled from the external tank. This also gives technicians enough time to fix any issue that might occur with the diesel filling system attached with the external tank.

Generator

External Diesel Tank

Standby generator fuel system is considered a mission-critical system for the Datacentre. As per the best practice, the generator fuel tank should be able to support the Datacentre design load for at least 12 hours. So, an external diesel tank of at least 5000 litres is typically installed for a moderate Datacentre. The external diesel tank is connected to the internal generator tank and is controlled by an automated concurrently maintainable or fault-tolerant filling system initialised automatically by the generator internal diesel level metre.

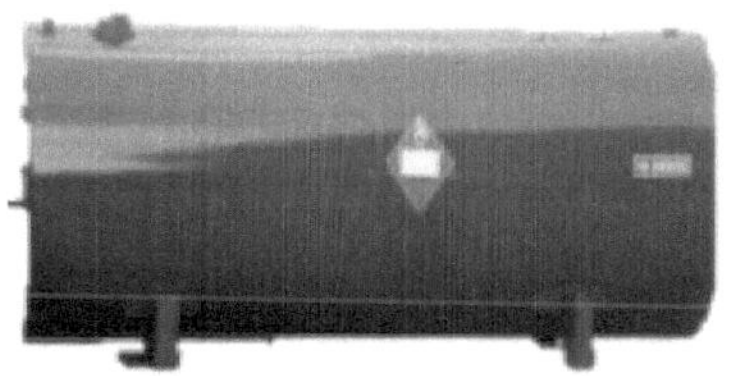

Fuel tank

IT IS RECOMMENDED TO install the external diesel tank higher than the generator level, as this allows to fuel the generator using the gravity via control valve such as a solenoid or motorised valve, instead of pumps. This reduces the faults chance.

Solenoid valve

Standby Generator Fuel Care

Diesel is an essential part of a "black start" exercise, so it needs special care. Black start is the process of restoring an electric power without relying on an external electric power source.

The diesel might stay in the standby generator for an extended period and this might cause some risks such as oxidation. Therefore, there should be a mechanism to keep the diesel clean and usable at all times. Usually, the diesel starts to deteriorate after six months, because of the issues listed below:

◇ Oxidation. It is a change in diesel components due to long periods of storage, which is usually over six months, and in some cases, up to a year.

◇ Bacterial action. This is the contamination of diesel by microbes such as bacteria and fungi.

◇ Sand, rust and water contamination. This can get into diesel because of condensation or adsorption from the air.

To overcome the above challenges, a particular diesel "washing" system can be used to clean the diesel and remove the diesel impurities. In all cases, the diesel must be replaced after two years, and the old clean diesel can be used for non-critical equipment such as cars.

Synchronisation Panel

Synchronisation panel is meant for running two or more DG sets in parallel on a common line while matching the characteristics of each system as closely as possible. This is generally used in case of inability of a single generator to supply the required power for the total load of the Datacentre. Hence, it can run two or more generators at the same time when necessary to provide the required load for the Datacentre.

Synchronisation panel

Automatic Transfer Switch (ATS)

ATS is a panel that detects when the mains electricity supply fails and trigger the standby generator control panel to start. Once ATS senses the electric power from the generator, it triggers the main breaker to transfer the Datacentre load to the generator. And when the main power comes back, ATS senses that and wait for a minute or two based on the configuration to make sure of the power stability. Then it disconnects the DG power and transfers the Datacentre load to the primary electricity grid. The generator continues to run for about 5 minutes without load to cool down before ATS sends a signal to it to shut down.

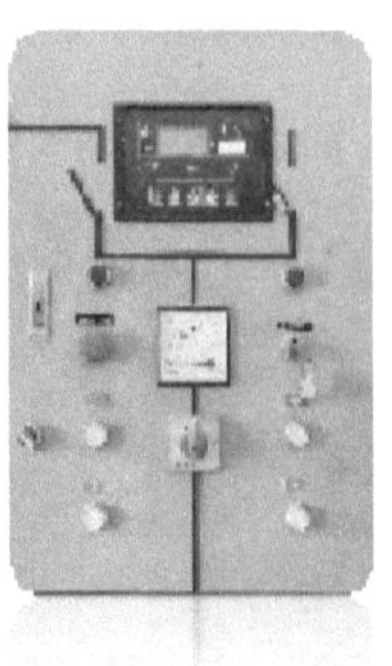

Automatic Transfer Switch

Uninterruptible Power Supply (UPS)

Even though the Datacentre is equipped with a standby generator that can provide electricity within few seconds, some equipment in the Datacentre can't withstand the disconnection of electricity for a second such as servers, network equipment, monitoring equipment and control equipment. Therefore, there should be a way to provide electrical power to these equipment immediately in case of a power failure and reduce their downtime to zero. Hence, UPS is essential to achieve this goal.

UNINTERRUPTIBLE POWER supply (UPS) is a power supply system that stores electric power in a battery. This stored power is supply to critical equipment in the event of a power surge or outage.

SINCE UPS ITSELF IS prone to faults, it is highly required to provide redundancy for it. So, two or more UPS should be installed on each line and each UPS capacity should be capable of handling the servers load. The redundant UPS needs to be installed in separate rooms for more safety in case of fire.

THE UPS RELIES ON DEEP cycle batteries to store energy, so it is recommended to install those batteries in isolated rooms for better safety. And those rooms have to be equipped with a ventilation system for better air quality since some types of batteries might generate some gases that can cause damages.

Uninterruptible Power Supply (UPS)

Isolate Server's UPS from Equipment's UPS

It is important to use a dedicated UPS for critical loads such as servers and network equipment loads and a separate UPS for other peripherals such as:

- ✓ Fire detection and extinguishing system.
- ✓ CCTV system.
- ✓ Access control system.
- ✓ Control room equipment and video walls.

Delta Conversion and Double Conversion UPS

Static UPS power conversion comes in two types. The first type is called Delta Conversion and the second type is called Double Conversion (On-Line UPS).

DELTA CONVERSION UPS moves much of the power from input to the output directly, as it is charging the battery and bypasses the power to the load. And when the primary powers cut off, it converts the Direct current (DC) from the battery to Alternating current (AC) and provides it to the load.

DOUBLE CONVERSION UPS converts AC to DC for the battery and back to AC for the load, so it is continuously converting AC to DC and DC to AC. When the main power line cut off, it converts the DC from the battery to AC and provides it to the load. This type is also called On-Line UPS as it maintains the power voltage level more effectively, so it works as a stabiliser for electric power.

UPS Battery

The batteries used for UPS are deep cycle batteries designed to discharge several times with minimal effect on its life. The forecasted lifespan of most of the batteries is 3 to 5 years under recommended conditions, and there are some long-life batteries available these days, but its cost is very high.

FOR BETTER BATTERY life, install them in isolated rooms, where proper ventilation can be provided using a ventilation system. The battery's ambient temperature must be 25°C (77°F), and the batteries should be closely monitored to detect any failure. This is because a single battery failure leads to a complete battery bank failure.

The battery bank consists of several batteries and the number of batteries is determined based on the total voltage required. Each battery is normally 12V, and the batteries in the bank are connected in series to multiply the voltage and get the required value for the bank. Then each bank is linked with the other in parallel.

UPS battery bank

UPS (Conventional vs Modular)

The static UPS has two main types, namely the conventional (the old type) and the modular (the new type). There are several differences between the two types but the most known are listed below:

Conventional UPS

- Requires more space as it is designed for full load from the onset.

- Has scalability issues if you need extra power, such as adding extra UPS that takes more space.

- Failure of modules leads to complete service interruption.

Modular UPS

- Save space as it requires less space for installation.

- Improve system reliability and availability.

- Hot-swappable modules to shorten the system installation and repair time.

- Better scalability. Easy to add more batteries when required.

- Each UPS can have built-in N+1 Redundant.

- Failure of modules might lead only to reduced UPS capacity.

- It provides optimised Capital Expenditure (CAPEX) and Operational Expenditure (OPEX).

Rotary UPS

Since static UPS relays on batteries, the batteries are subject to failure after a few years, and the cost of batteries and its maintenance is very high. In order to eliminate these issues, the rotary UPS was introduced, which came with a better solution.

Rotary UPS is an electric generator connected to a flywheel and a clutch and then connected to a diesel generator.

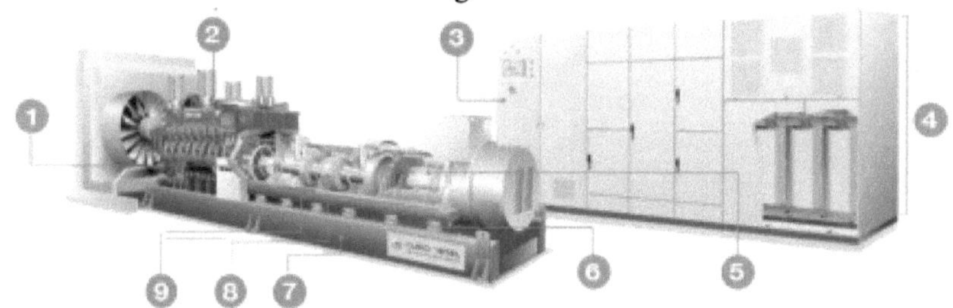

Rotary UPS

Image from Standby Power Generation UK Limited (standbypowergeneration.co.uk)

1. Electromagnetic Clutch.
2. Diesel Engines.
3. KS-VISION (user-friendly touch-screen HMI).
4. Power Panels (switch gears and chokes).
5. 4-Pole Synchronous Machine.
6. Built-in Vibration Dampers.
7. Monobloc (rigid assembly).
8. Kinetic Energy Accumulator.
9. Brushless Exciter.

This system keeps rotating continuously, and when the main electrical power cuts off, the electrical load is transferred to the generator that continues to rotate as a result of the weight of the rotating flywheel. At this time, the diesel engine would start working, and the clutch connects the generator to the diesel engine to continue generating electricity until the main electricity returns. This way, the electricity is not cut off from the Datacentre even for a second. The advantages of rotary UPS are as follows:

- Eliminate the need for battery as energy storage.
- Eliminate battery maintenance cost.
- Eliminate the risk of battery failure.
- Avoid the cooling interruption on-grid failure.

Power Distribution Unit (PDU)

PDU, also called by some as Power strip, is an essential part of the electric power distribution. Each server cabinet has two of them, and each one is connected to independent electricity line for redundancy. Each server or network appliance is connected to both of the strips and comes in several types. The characteristics of these types can be summarised as follows:

1. **Basic type**: This is a dummy strip without any intelligence.

2. **Metered type**: This strip is equipped with a power meter that displays the total load on the strip. It is useful to make sure that the load doesn't exceed the capability of the strip.

3. **Monitored type**: This strip is an intelligent device that is connected to the data network where the admins can monitor the load on each device remotely. Usually, these strips are monitored via special software provided by the manufacturer or via Datacentre Infrastructure Management System (DCIM) if available.

4. **Switched type**: This strip is also monitored remotely like the Monitored type, but it is much advanced as it can be switched on and off remotely via the data network so that the technician can manage the power switches remotely. This type of strips requires a qualified administrator who understand what he is doing very well, as this can shut down

any device with the touch of a button. This type of strips is highly useful for remote Datacentres.

Power Distribution Unit

Industrial Plug Sockets

Industrial plugs and sockets provide a connection to electrical mains. It is specially designed for advance usage, unlike household plugs and sockets. Server cabinets are connected to the electricity supply via industrial sockets. Also, the old usual cabling method or the new bus-bar method uses industrial sockets to connect the server cabinets. Industrial connectors can be a single-phase for ordinary systems or three-phase for large systems.

Industrial connector

Traditional Power Cabling

• Each server cabinet requires 2 Cables from the Remote Power Panel (RPP).

• To change the supply from a single-phase to three-phase, a cable replacement is required and it requires extra space for three-phase breaker in the RPP.

• The RPP size is fixed from the onset, so if it is already full, then you need a new one which is a mini project by itself.

• Expansion is possible with a limit, and the limit is the available space in the RPP.

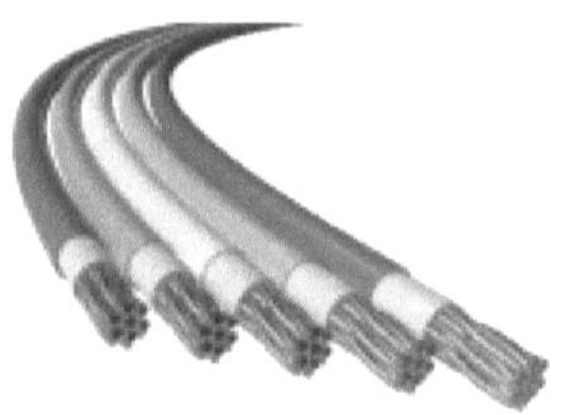

Traditional Cables

Electrical Bus-bar Power Distribution

Bus-bar system is the industry-leading electrical power distribution system for the Datacentre/mission-critical and industrial markets. This system is the best for Datacentres due to its unique characteristics.

THE ELECTRICAL BUS-bar system is a way of delivering electric power to the cabinets using customised tap-off boxes directly fitted to a current-carrying bus-bar with a variety of power requirements regardless of the brand. The tap-off can be a single-phase or three-phase, 16Amps, 32Amps, and you are not limited to a specific type or size.

THIS SYSTEM IS ENTIRELY modular and is easy to be monitored and managed via TCP IP connection, which is available in each tap-off box. The most important advantages of this system are speed installation and flexibility, modularity, and transformability.

Bus-bar system

———◉———

TIP : *Bus-bar system is the best option available as it provides reliability, ease of maintenance, security, and scalability for the future.*

Maintenance Bypass Switch

Manual maintenance bypass switches are essential to allow service and isolation for safety purposes. Electrical systems should enable these operations to be performed without causing loss of power. For example, maintaining the UPS, isolator switches or cable connectors requires disconnection of power from these lines. At the same time, it is required to provide an alternative route for the ability to maintain the redundancy all the time.

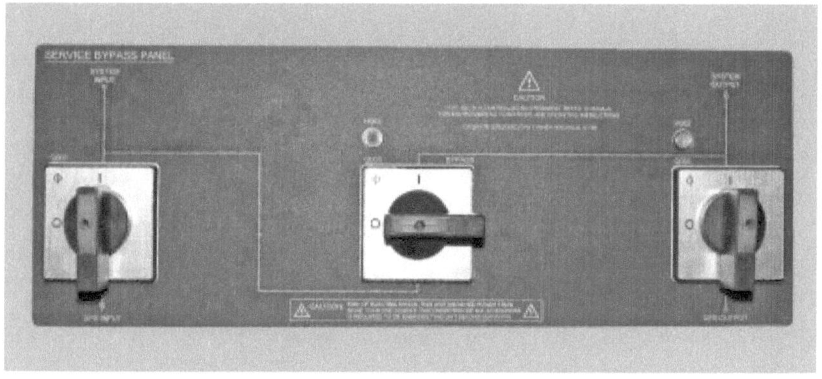

Manual maintenance bypass switches

The Most Typical Four Datacentre Tiers

The most public used Datacentre tiers are Tier 1, Tier 2, Tier 3, and Tier 4. Each tier has specific characteristics and reliability, and this is reflected in the cost of the Datacentre.

Tier 1 Datacentre is the cheapest design. It has no redundancy and can be presented as follows:

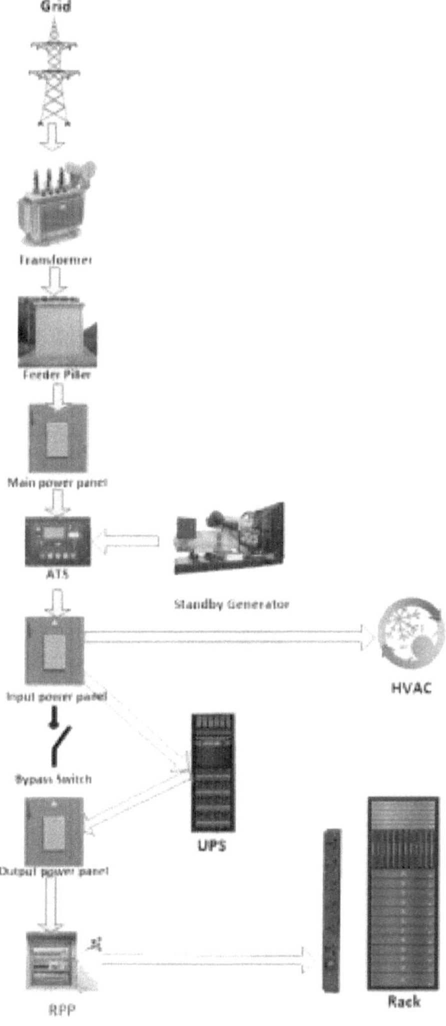

TIER 2 HAS SOME REDUNDANCY for the critical load but still has a single source of primary power and a standby generator.

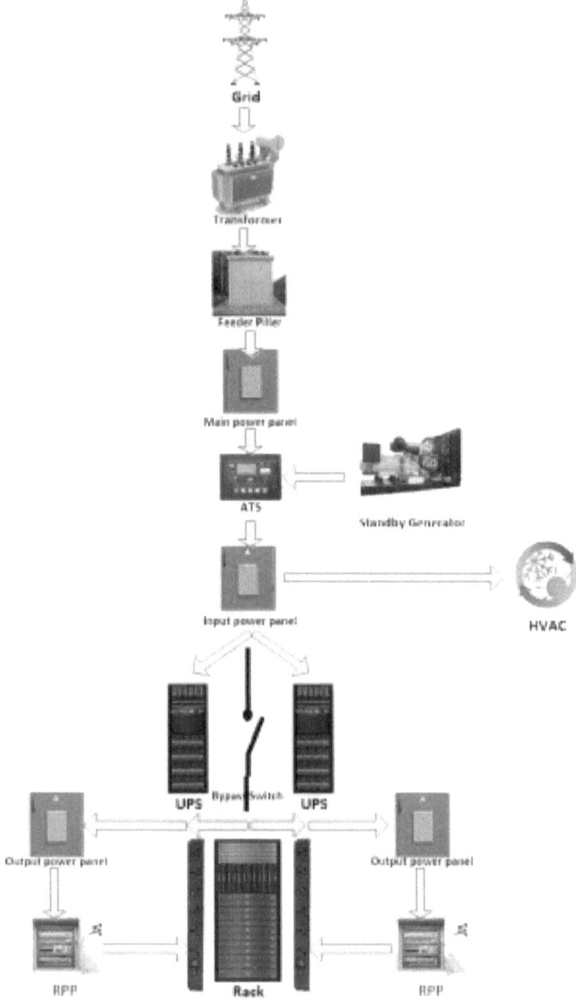

TIER 3 HAS REASONABLE redundancy for critical load and mechanical load. It might have redundant standby generators but still has one primary grid. An extra UPS can be added for HVAC system pumps and blowers as an option.

Typical Tier 3 redundant datacenter

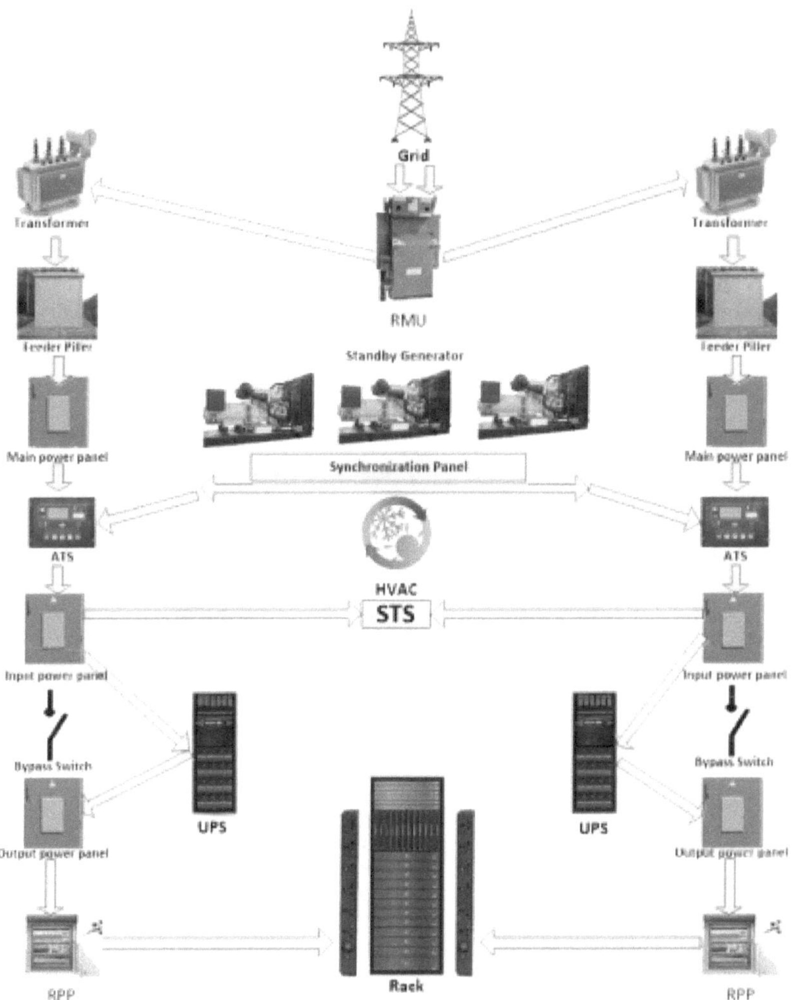

Tier 4 is the best and the most costly design. This is because it guarantees the availability of two isolated redundant power supply.

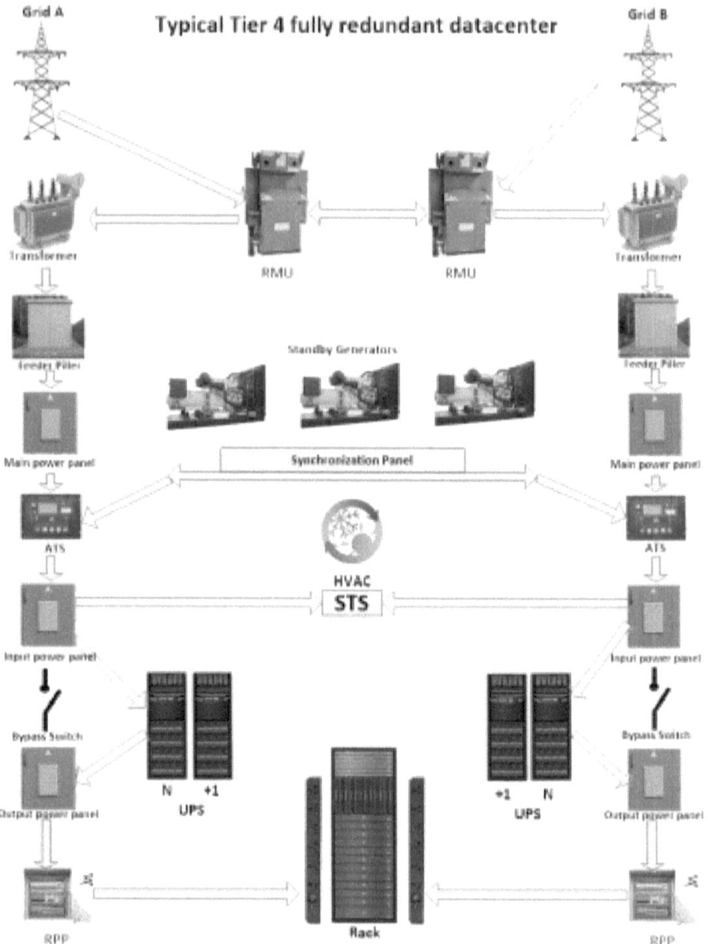

IN TIER 4 EACH POWER line has all of the standard requirements such as transformer, feeder pillar, standby generator, Dual UPS, ATS and RPP. An Extra UPS can be added for HVAC system pumps and blowers as an option.

The cooling system is equipped with Static Transfer Switch (STS) that provides power from one of the available lines and immediately transfers the cooling/heating load to the alternative line in no time. There is no harm if these systems go down during the power transformation from the grid to a standby generator, which does not exceed 25 to 45 seconds. This scenario can happen if both grids go down, which happens in rare cases.

<hr>

TIP : *For more reliability, the designer can add an extra UPS to supply the cooling pumps and air blowers. This is useful especially with the chiller cooling system, as it can make use of the availability of cold water to continue the Datacentre cooling until the generators take up the load.*

Electricity Rooms and Cable Paths

1. The Datacentre typically has two electricity rooms. These electricity rooms must be separated, and for best design, they must be located on both sides of the Datacentre building.

---

2. Transformers fed by different networks must be wholly separated to ensure the best safety and reliability.

---

3. The main LV cable should be routed in two different paths to guarantee that damaging any line does not affect both lines.

---

4. Main cables must be protected and marked on the ground to provide a clear warning for future maintenance and to protect the cables against illegal excavation.

Electricity room

Emergency Power Off (EPO)

Emergency power off is a type of control mechanism for an emergency power supply or "generator" meant to disconnect power and shut down the Datacentre/Device.

It is a safety mechanism in case the primary disconnect device is not readily accessible due to a fire or other unsafe condition. This switch may be available for the standby generator and can also be installed in the Datacentre.

Emergency power off switch

Datacentre Earthing

The Signal Reference Grid (SRG) is a network of copper wires typically installed below the raised floor in the Datacentre. All of the raised floor pillars are connected to this network.

The goal of this network is the safe disposal of static electricity that may form for any reason and is a network independent of the ground network of other electrical connections.

***

EARTH ROD IS MADE OF copper and is the part that is buried at a depth of 4 feet in the ground. To increase the efficiency of the connectivity of the earth rod, we have to add the following to the ground pillar hole:

- **Charcoal.** It contains carbon and serves the purpose of a perfect conductor.

- **Salt.** Salt is used as an electrolyte to form conductivity between GI plate coal and earth with humidity.

- **The mixture of both** has to be watered regularly to increase its conductivity.

Earth Rod

Electricity Safety and Precautions

1. Always use fire-rated cables in the Datacentre.

2. Make sure the server cabinet earthing is isolated from other earthing.

3. The raised floor must be earthed using Signal Reference Grid (SRG).

4. The cables must be routed on a cable tray either under the raised floor or above the cabinets.

5. All cables must be labelled with a long-lasting material such as aluminium plate, as this is important for future maintenance.

6. All electricity cabinets must be labelled clearly.

7. All electricity cabinets must have a danger warning, especially the high voltage one.

8. The transformers and generators area must be protected with a wall or steel fence.

Lighting and Signage

The lighting inside the Datacentre needs to be controlled with an occupancy sensor. The sensor detects the presence of people in the target-monitored area. The lighting is switched on in the presence of a human being. The occupancy sensor is not the same as the motion sensor. The difference between them is that the occupancy sensor produces signals whether an object is stationary or not while the motion sensor is sensitive to only moving objects.

***

TIP : *All rooms and departments in the Datacentre require a name board. Exit paths signs are also necessary because they are part of safety precautions. In general, all equipment in the Datacentre must contain an operating instruction board, especially the emergency equipment.*

Chapter 7 Datacentre Electric/Cooling Load Calculation

Electrical Power Requirement

To correctly design the electrical system, it is essential to calculate the total load of the Datacentre. To achieve this, we need to know the required electrical load, and then we can decide, the size of the transformer, the size of the standby generator, the size of the UPS, and the cooling capacity. There are different calculations methods and the designer can choose the one that he/she prefers. However, choosing the right formula depends on the availability of information. If you do not have detailed information about the types of equipment to be installed, then the below-described approach is recommended.

First, you need to find out the white space area in metre, the current expected number of cabinets, the number of future cabinets, and the cabinet's maximum expected power requirement in watt. For example, if the area is 20x15 metres, the currently expected cabinets are 16, the future cabinets are 10, and the maximum cabinet power requirement is 5000W = 5KW, then the calculation is as follows:

A. Area= Room Length 20m x Width 15m = 300m².
B. Number of cabinets (Current) = 16 Cabinets.
C. Number of cabinets (Future) = 10 Cabinets.
D. Cabinet maximum power requirement (watt) = 5000W

The critical load value

Rating of each IT device = (Calculate total in watt x 0.67)/1000
E. (B*D *0.67)/1000 = (16*5000 *0.67)/1000 = <u>53.6 KW</u>

Load value for the equipment not listed in the sizing calculator, critical load – nameplate

Subtotal volt-amps (VA) include fire, security and monitoring systems
F. (D x 0.67)/1000 = (5000 x 0.67)/1000 = <u>3.350 KW</u>

Future loads value

G. [(C x D) x 0.67]/1000 = [(10 x 5000) x 0.67]/1000 = <u>33.5 KW</u>

Peak power draw due to variation in critical loads (total steady state critical load power draw)

H. (E + F + G) x 1.05 = (53.6+3.350+33.5)x1.05= <u>94.97</u> <u>KW</u>

UPS inefficiency and battery charging (Actual Load + Future Load "in KW")

I. (E + F + G) x 0.32 = (53.6+3.350+33.5)x 0.32 = <u>28.944KW</u>

Lighting (Total floor area associated with the Datacentre)

J. 0.0215 x floor area (sqm) = 0.0215 x A = 0.0215 x 300 = <u>6.45KW</u>

Size of standby UPS estimate (Total power to support electrical demands)

K. (H+ I + F) = (94.97+28.944+3.350)= <u>127.264 KW</u>
Convert KW to KVA = (127.264 x 1.25) = **159.08 KVA**

Power requirement for cooling (Total power to support cooling demands)

L. For Chiller systems, K x 0.7. For DX systems K x 1.0. We adopt chiller system, so 159.08 x 0.7 = <u>111.356 KW</u>

Total power to support electrical and cooling demands

M. (K + L) = (159.08 + 111.356) = <u>270.436 KW</u>

Requirements to meet National Electrical Code (NEC) and other regulators

N. (M x 1.25) = 270.436 x 1.25 = <u>338.045KW</u>

O. Three-phase AC voltage provided at service entrance = 415VAC (This is UK standard)

Note: the United States and Canada standard is 208VAC.

Electrical service required from the utility company in Amps

P. ((N x 1000)/(O x 1.73)) = (338.045 x 1000)/(415 x 1.73) = 470.848Amps

Size of Standby Generator Estimate

Q. Critical loads requiring generator back up = (K x 1.3) = 159.08 x 1.3 = 206.804 KW

WARNING: The 1.3 variable applies to fully power factor corrected UPS. A 3.0 multiplier must be used when using traditional UPS with harmonic input filters.

R. Cooling loads requiring generator back up (L x 1.5) = 111.356 x 1.5 = 167.034 KW

S. Size of generator needed (Q + R) = (206.804 + 167.034) = 373.838 KW

T. Size of generator needed in KVA = (S x 1.25) = (373.838 x 1.25) = 467.298 KVA

Finally, from the above calculation, it appears that the following capacities are required for the above Datacentre:

I. UPS capacity: 159.08 KVA.
II. Cooling Capacity: 111.356 KW.
In Tons = (111.356 KW/3.5168) =31.664 Tons of cooling.
III. Generator Capacity: 467.298 KVA

IV. Grid Capacity: 470.848 Amps = 338.446 KVA.

Chapter 8: Network Design

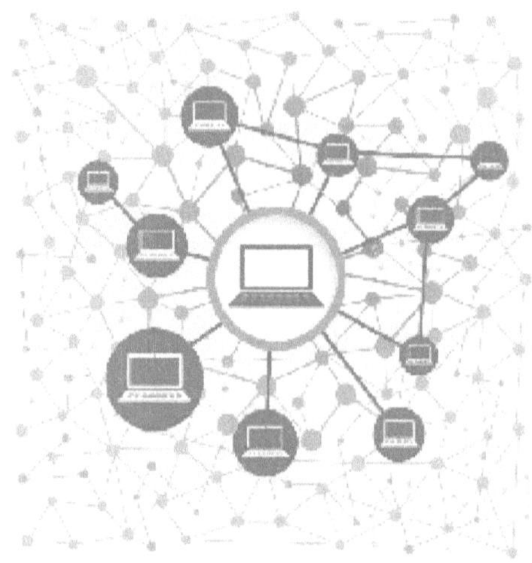

Network Design Guidance

Designing the Datacentre network is crucial. Networking technology is developing very quickly, so the network design must be done by a person that is familiar with the latest developments in this field.

WHILE DESIGNING THE network, emphasise on cabling architecture and keep an eye toward future growth and scalability.

Following this advice helps to make the Datacentre scalable as the primary goal of the modern designs is to accommodate future growth and emerging technologies. It is also essential to consider the quality of the cables and appliances used in the networks. Always think of the compatibility between the multiple available manufacturers and never put your neck in the hands of any manufacturer.

***

PAY CLOSE ATTENTION to organising and proper documentation; this is always the biggest challenge. Most of the implementers do not make reasonable efforts in preparing proper documentation, and the client also does not focus on the importance of these documentations. These documentations are essential for the future. You are coming to know how important is it when your current employees leave the work and the new employees do not know how the network was designed and what it entails. Besides, the auditors might ask for these documentations to accomplish their job.

Network Cabling Infrastructure

Avoid Spaghetti. One of the common challenges in Datacentres is the so-called network cables spaghetti, but what do we mean by this? It means that the network cables are tangled in a way that it is impossible to know where the cable comes from and where it is going to. The cables might also be mix with telephone and electricity cables which make it worse. This happens because over time, technicians may replace some cables with other cables without removing the old ones due to their intertwining with other cables. So, the matter of removing them becomes dangerous since there is a risk of causing other problems. The question is, why does this happen? This happens as a result of a wrong network design with no proper labelling and colour-coding, along with carelessness of network technician and unfollowing up of the Datacentre manager. The Datacentre might reach this point in no time.

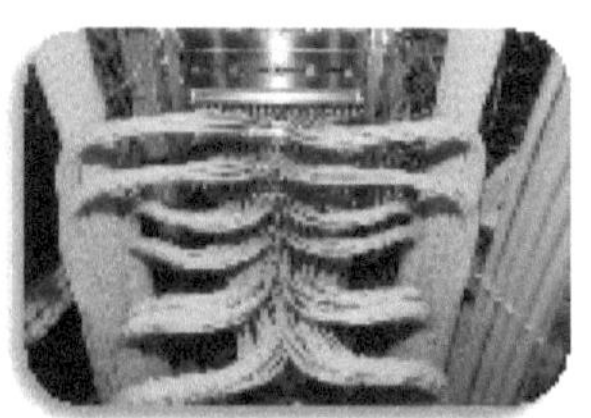

Organised Cabling

IT IS ESSENTIAL TO consider the following points to keep the Datacentre away from network cables spaghetti:

◈ **Use Cable tray:** It is always essential to use a separate tray for each service such as electricity, telephone, and network. This keeps the cables organised and separated from each other. The electricity cables need to be away from other cables to avoid any interference that might affect the quality of service.

Cable tray

◈ **Follow colour coding:** Colour coding is highly essential, especially for the same cable type such as networks cables that can serve multiple services, e.g., LAN, Internet or Integrated Lights-Out (ILO) cables. Therefore, it is essential to use a different colour for each set of cables to make it easy to identify.

Coloured coded cables

◇ **Labelling:** Every cable needs labelling in both ends for easy identification and the label needs to be of acceptable quality that can last long periods. The label should contain the cable type and its serial number and should be easy to read. It is essential to refer to the Cable Labelling Standards ANSI TIA 606-B as it guides on how to label IT environment cables in the right way. Labelling is essential for future maintenance.

Network cables labelling

◇ **Internal Agreement** - There should be an internal agreement among all departments and team members; everybody needs to agree to follow these standards strictly. Otherwise, it will only create additional confusion.

Intelligent Infrastructure Management (IIM)

I t is well known that data network technologies are developing very quickly, as we now have smart networks that facilitate the management process and fix errors, or even avoid them before they happen. The Intelligent Infrastructure Management is a technology launch that integrates a powerful combination of innovative Smart Patch Panels, user-friendly Master Control Panels and software that provides real-time monitoring and reporting of network-wide physical layer activity. It is recommended to go for this type of networks if the budget allocated for the project could accommodate the cost.

Chapter 9: Security Systems

Importance of Security System

The security system is one of the most critical pillars of Datacentre. It is designed to guarantee the security and safety of the Datacentre components and workers. Therefore, the designer should pay special attention to this system. The Datacentre security system consists of the following components:

Physical access control. It is a matter of controlling who, where, and when. This system is essential to control the physical security of the Datacentre, where it protects each room of the Datacentre from any illegal access. Electronic access control uses computer software to solve the limitations of mechanical locks and keys, which makes doors management much easier and smooth.

Security System

THE ELECTRONIC COMPUTERISED access control system grants access based on the credential presented by the admin. A wide range of credentials can be used to replace traditional mechanical keys. The access control can use a Pin Code, fingerprint, RFID Card, Eye Recognition, Vein Recognition, Face recognition and Microchip Implant.

The Datacentre needs to have robust physical security features. These characteristics prevent any activity that may compromise the security of the Datacentre. Below is a list of some of the features that can be integrated within the access control system.

DOOR INTERLOCK. It is a way to guarantee that two interlocked doors can't be opened at the same time. This mechanism can be used for the main whitespace area entrance, as it helps to keep the cold air inside the room and is one of the access control mechanism that allows only one person to access at a time. When an employee opens the first door, nobody can open the second door. Also, the employee himself cannot open the second door until the first door is closed.

ANTI-PASSBACK. It is a mechanism to guarantee that the employee who accesses the door can only get out of that door. Still, if he/she has not entered from the same door, he/she cannot open the door to go out. A warning can be fired off to notify the security officer. The idea behind this is to guarantee that when an employee enters through an assigned door, he/she should also exit through the same door. This ensures recording the accurate access and exit time of the employee for future investigation if required or even for attendance registration.

MULTI-FACTOR AUTHENTICATION. It is a mechanism to secure access to the door with more than one factor. For example, the user should simultaneously use Radio Frequency Identification (RFID) card and password to open the door or fingerprint along with the RFID card and pin code.

Multi-factor authentication

DURESS PIN. It is a four-digit code used to send "distress signal" to the security officer. It is used by the employee if he is forced by an intruder to open the door. This PIN opens the door and sends a silent distress alarm to the security office.

Access Control Electric Lock Types

- **Strike lock**. It is a lock that comes as Normally Open (NO) or Normally Closed (NC). It requires Cylindrical Door Lock Latch Tongue to be installed in the door.

Strike lock

- **Electromagnetic lock.** It is a lock that comes as NC. This is widely used for access control, and it doesn't require any modifications in the door. It comes in different power capacity, the most widely used is the 180Kg Holding Force.

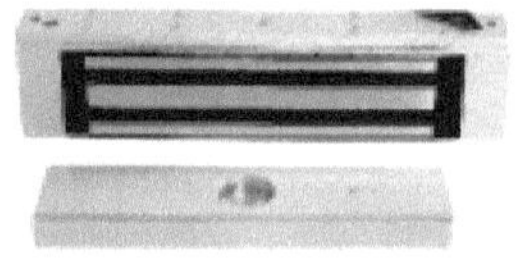

Electromagnetic lock

- **Rim Lock.** This lock is typically used in metal doors and not widely used in the Datacentre. It comes as NO type. This lock can be opened via a mechanical key along with the electricity. The characteristic of this lock is that it opens once it gets electrical power; otherwise, it remains closed.

Rim Lock

• **Deadbolt Lock**. This lock comes in two types: one on the surface installation and the other is concealed in the door. It is usually NC type, but it comes as NO also. One of the models is equipped with a mechanical key and is usually installed by concealing in the door.

Deadbolt Lock

Access Control Reader Types

- **Radio Frequency Identification (RFID) card reader**. This reader can read the RFID cards that come in different frequencies.

RFID card reader

- **PIN keypad**. This type has a pressable numeric key. It accepts only a PIN code. The pin code length differs based on the user requirements.

PIN Keypad

- **Fingerprint reader**. It is a reader that can read the user's fingerprint and send it to the central controller for authentication and authorisation.

Fingerprint reader

• **Eye Recognition device**. This device has iris recognition scanners, illuminating the iris with infrared light to pick up the unique patterns that are not visible to the human eye.

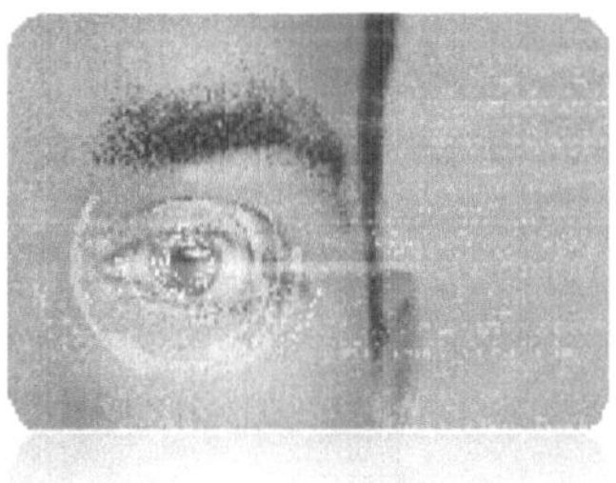

Eye recognition

• **Vein Recognition**. This is a scanner that takes a digital picture of the hand veins using near-infrared light where the blood absorbs the light. Hence, veins appear black in the picture, and each person has different veins structure which is used as a user identifier.

Vein recognition

• **Face recognition**. It is a system of using biometrics to map facial features to differentiate between individuals and can be used to authenticate users.

Face recognition

Future Physical Security

The next evolution will be employees being implanted with a microchip. By injecting this tiny microchip into the employee's hand, all kinds of data can be programmed, and this allows the employee just to pass his/her hand on the reader to access the authorised room. This technology guarantees that the employee has his access permit with him all the time; it works well against ID theft.

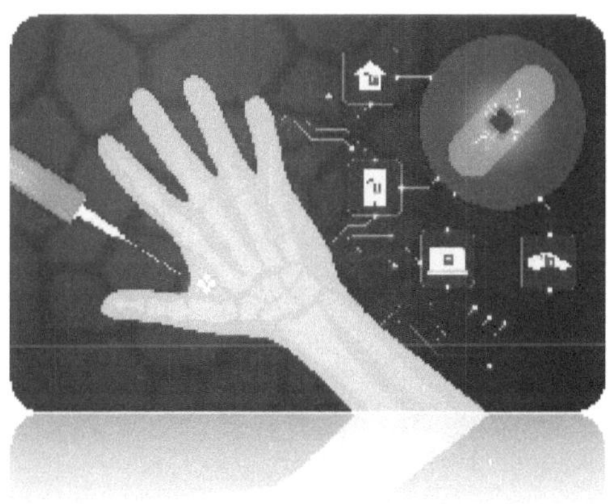

Body implanted microchip

Access Control and Fire Alarm System Integration

Standard fire codes such as National Fire Protection Association (NFPA 75) designate that all the electric locks should immediately open on the sound of a fire alarm to provide free access and exit. Therefore, you need to choose the equivalent access control that supports this vital feature.

Surveillance and Monitoring system

The video surveillance and monitoring system is an integral part of Datacentres' physical security posture. Hence, it is highly required to pay special attention when designing the system to use the right camera for the right place and make sure to avoid any blind area.

Monitoring Cameras

COMMON ISSUES:

1. **Cloudy or obstructed cameras**. Choosing the right camera is an essential part to guarantee clear video and images. Therefore, always choose a Closed-Circuit Television (CCTV) company that is certificated to meet the required security field standards.

2. **Clocks accuracy.** CCTV recording relies heavily on time, either for recording or retrieving the recorded video. Wrong timing can cause several problems that can lead to losing crucial required evidence. Therefore, the CCTV system must be synchronised with an authoritative Network Time Protocol (NTP) server.

3. **Operating systems maintainability**. Always make sure to use a CCTV system on a new operating system that can get updated from the originator. This is very important for an efficient CCTV system that runs smoothly and with minimal failure.

4. **Video retention capability.** The calculation of the required storage for the required period with a particular recording quality is an essential part of the beginning. The quality of cameras plays an integral part for the calculation, and it is always recommended to add some buffer for new cameras that can be added in the near future. On average, keeping recording for 90 days is recommended.

Surveillance System Recommendations

1. **Network Video Recorder (NVR) redundancy.** It is always recommended to use a failover system for the CCTV system. This can be achieved by using dual NVRs. If one NVR fails, the second takes over the load and it should failback automatically once the main NVR issue is fixed.

2. **Use reliable NVR.** It usually comes as a ready-made box with its operating system, or it can be just a special software installed on any powerful server provided from any manufacturer. It is possible to use NVR box for small scale up to 256 channel. The advantage of this device is the cost perfection, reliability as it is made and tested, and supports ease of management and maintenance.

3. **Use surveillance Hard Disk**. Usually, NVR uses Serial Advanced Technology Attachment (SATA) hard disks unless it is an extensive system which relays on Storage Area Network (SAN) or Network Attached Storage (NAS). SAN/NAS can use disks that are built explicitly for these environments, which can be SATA, Small Computer System Interface (SCSI) or Solid State Drive (SSD) hard disks. SATA hard disks are used widely for small to medium CCTV systems. It comes in several types; one of these types is specially designed for surveillance systems as it supports 80% writing and 20% reading. It is the optimal setup for NVR as it is continuous writing, but reading is only required when retrieving recording. Surveillance hard disks are

designed to work 24/7. It has a long lifespan, so always use surveillance hard disk and not standard desktop hard disks.

Hard Disk

4. **Redundant Array of Inexpensive Disks (RAID) System.** Always select an NVR which supports RAID, as it is the technology that provides more reliability. Nowadays, most of the advanced NVRs support different types of RAIDS such as RAID 0,1, 5,6 and 10.

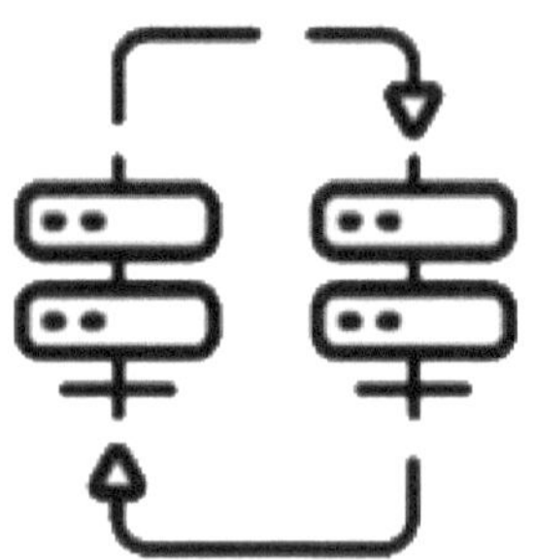

RAID System

a. **RAID0** is ideal for non-critical storage and offers excellent performance, but not fault-tolerant.

b. **RAID1** data are stored twice by writing them to both disk drives at the same time. It provides fault-tolerant but limited in the number of hard disks and space and its costly solution.

c. **RAID5** requires at least 3 drives, and data is distributed among the hard disks but one hard disk stores the data checksum writing in all of the hard disks. The system is not broken due to failure of one hard disk, and can simply replace the defective hard disk without any loss of data.

d. **RAID6** is similar to RAID5, but it is writing the data checksum to two drives. This means that it requires at least 4 drives as a start. The system is not broken due to failure of even two hard drives, and can simply replace the defective hard drives without any loss of data.

e. **RAID10** is merging between the idea of RAID0 and RAID1, where it comes over the advantages/disadvantages of RAID0 and RAID1. It has the most expensive way to have redundancy as half of the storage capacity goes to mirroring.

5. **The right camera for the right purpose.** The cameras come in several shapes; each serves a purpose and is designed to work in a specific environment. Therefore, always use the right camera in the right place to get the expected result. Besides, consider the angle, shades, blind-spot and objects when designing a CCTV system.

6. **Use UPS to support the system**. CCTV system is one of the critical systems in the Datacentre. Therefore, it should be supported by UPS, and the UPS should also support all

of the connected switches to avoid any failure in case of electrical power failure.

TIP : *It appears that RAID5 and RAID6 are the most suitable RAIDs for the NVR systems, so make sure to choose an NVR that supports at least those two, or just relay on NAS to store your surveillance data.*

Types of CCTV Cameras

• **Dome Camera**. Dome cameras are either attached to the ceiling or hung on a special wall-mount. That's depending on the target and the required field of view. The dome of the camera is usually transparent and can be black if it is required to hide the direction of the camera.

Dome Camera

• **Bullet Camera**. It is named Bullet due to its distinctive cylindrical shape, and is usually used in outdoor.

Bullet Camera

• **Fisheye Camera**. A Fisheye lens is an ultra-wide-angle lens that provides 360° panoramic or hemispherical image. The image can either be displayed as one panoramic image or split into several standard views. It is generally installed in the middle of the room, and recently, the outdoor Bullet cameras are equipped with the same lenses.

Fisheye Camera

• **Varifocal camera**. This can be any type of camera equipped with a varifocal lens that can zoom in and out. It captures a broader or narrow area with more detail. It usually comes with a 2.8-12mm lens, and the largest is 5-100mm. The camera comes in two main types; the first has fixed varifocal, which is configured on installation while the second is motorised—it can be controlled remotely through the software at any time.

• **PTZ camera**. Pan-tilt-zoom (PTZ) is the name given to the camera that is capable of moving in all directions. The user can also control the zoom and focus of the lens. The image can be zoomed several times, depending on the efficiency of the camera. The camera supports preset zones where it automatically moves and focus on the preset zone for a preconfigured time and then move to the second zone automatically.

PTZ Camera

- **Thermal Camera**. A thermal imaging camera is a type of thermographic camera. This camera displays the heat of living creatures or fire by rendering infrared radiation. It can work through smoke or fog; the high-temperature objects appear in red colour.

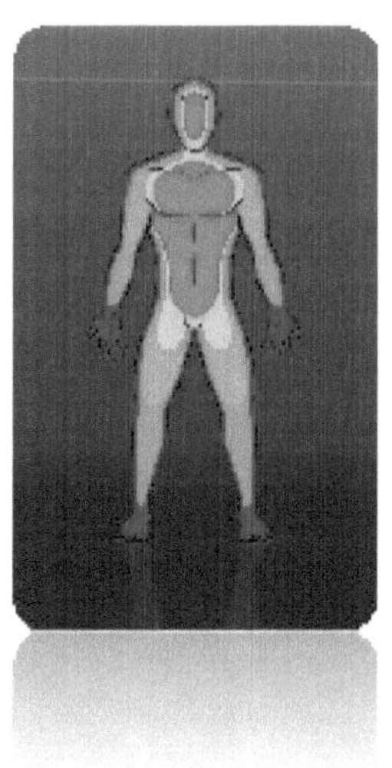

Thermal Camera image

• **ANPR Camera**. This camera is used to recognise cars' registration plate numbers, with the help of particular software. It uses optical character recognition on images, extracts the characters/numbers and converts them into digital form. It can compare a car plate number to a number stored in the database, or just store it in the database in case of logging. This camera can be used to open car gates for permitted cars or identify cars for the daily police operation. It is worth mentioning that the number recognition feature may be a software and works with any advanced camera with high accuracy.

• **Body Temperature Measurement Camera**. This camera uses thermal imaging for detecting elevated body temperature. The camera can detect multiple people temperature at the same time; it shows each person's temperature. It can fire a warning on detecting a person with high temperature and send an email to a specific email address. Also, the efficacy of the camera can reach up to 9 meters.

Body Temperature Measurement Process

CCTV Advanced Features

• **Facial Recognition System**. Facial recognition system is a way to identify a person through biometrics map facial features using his photograph or video. This system can be used to open doors for the authorised persons without touching anything. It can also be used for employees attendance and in airports to identify suspicious persons. This technology relies typically on software rather than a camera, and most of the high definitions camera can work with this system.

Facial Recognition System

• **Object Detection**. Object detection system is a powerful camera supported by a computer software technology related to computer vision and image processing that deals with detecting instances of objects. It is used to discover missing items or newly added items and is used in sensitive places such as Datacentres and airports.

• **Cross Line Detection**. It is a camera with an application primarily used for general entrance and exit detection in low-traffic areas. The system can fire a warning or start recording once somebody crosses the virtual line, or it can count the number of people crossing the line.

IP Cameras Specifications

Megapixel: This is a general term used for any camera that has over 1 million pixels in the sensor; there are 1.0, 2.0, 3.0, 5, 8, 10 and higher megapixel cameras. This is one of the essential specifications of a camera. Typically, 4 megapixel is fair enough for standard surveillance needs. 4K that is equal to about 8.5 megapixels widely spread nowadays.

RESOLUTION: 720p cameras usually have a sensor with at least 1.0 megapixels and pixel resolution is 1280 x 1024. 1080p cameras have at least a 2-megapixel sensor and pixel resolution is 1920×1080, also known as Full HD. 4K camera usually refers to a camera with over 8 megapixels of resolution.

MINIMUM ILLUMINATION: It is the lowest light level that provides a good image from the IP camera.

LENS ANGLE: The lens allows you to frame the area that you want to see. The lower the size, the wider the viewing angle.

- 2.8 mm horizontal FOV: 103°, vertical FOV: 58°, diagonal FOV: 123°

- 4 mm horizontal FOV: 83°, vertical FOV: 45°, diagonal FOV: 99°

- 6 mm horizontal FOV: 51°, vertical FOV: 29°, diagonal FOV: 58°

- 8 mm horizontal FOV: 39°, vertical FOV: 22°, diagonal FOV: 45°

Iris: Iris control adjusts how much light is allowed to fall on the sensor; this helps the camera to show a perfect image regardless of the amount of available light.

WIDE DYNAMIC RANGE (WDR): This technology improves the overall image quality on dark and bright areas as it creates a balance to improve the overall image quality.

Public Address System

Public address and voice evacuation system is essential for dealing with security and safety challenges. Therefore, it is necessary to install PA system inside the Datacentre. It can be used for direct instruction or evacuation call in case of emergency. It can also be connected to the fire alarm system where it works as a warning siren. The system should support zoning so that the user can choose a specific zone for the call or all of the zones. The calling points can be in the Datacentre management office and the security office.

PA System

Chapter 10: Monitoring and Control

Environment Monitoring

Monitoring the environment of the Datacentre is an essential part of the Datacentre. This process keeps the Datacentre working in the best possible conditions because by monitoring, the faults can be fixed immediately and failures will be avoided.

What are the things to monitor?

A. **Temperature and humidity.** These are the most critical environmental elements that need to be monitored strictly. The monitoring system needs to concentrate on the servers temperature rather than the room temperature. This is because the white space is not considered a comfort zone for human, unlike the servers that are the most critical element in the Datacentre.

B. **Airflow.** The airflow needs to be monitored from two points, namely the inlet and return air ducts. This monitoring can give a good indicator on the level of the airflow efficiency. If the difference between the incoming and outgoing air is enormous, then there is an issue. If this occurs, it may cause cooling inefficiency, and consequently, bad Power Usage Effectiveness (PUE).

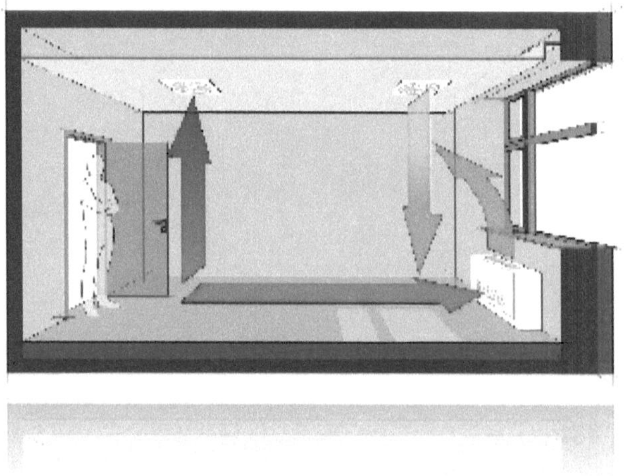

Cooling Airflow

C. **Water leakage**. It is considered as one of the critical hazards to be monitored. Water leakage is a dangerous hazard, so it needs to be monitored using a water leakage detector that is generally installed below the raised floor. The most critical areas to be monitored are the areas below the Computer Room Air Conditioning (CRAC) units. This is because the CRAC units might work with chilled water, and might also have built-in humidifiers that are equipped with a water source to generate humidity when required. Dehumidifier also needs to be monitored since it collects the humidity and drains it as water through the drainage pipes. This monitoring can prevent a disaster from happening in case of a dangerous flood that might come from the outside of the Datacentre.

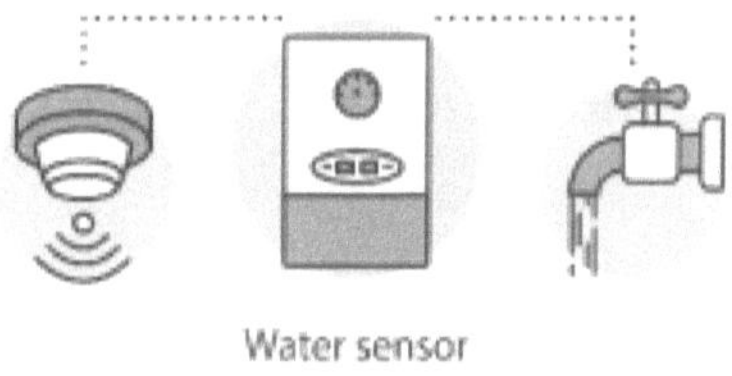

Water Leakage Detector

D. **Physical access doors**. These doors need to be monitored via an access control system in order to maintain the security of the Datacentre. Keeping the main door opened for a long time can cause cooling system troubles and dust can leak into the white space. Also, it gives a chance to unauthorised personnel to enter the Datacentre. The server cabinet doors also need to be monitored to guarantee that only authorised personnel can maintain the servers.

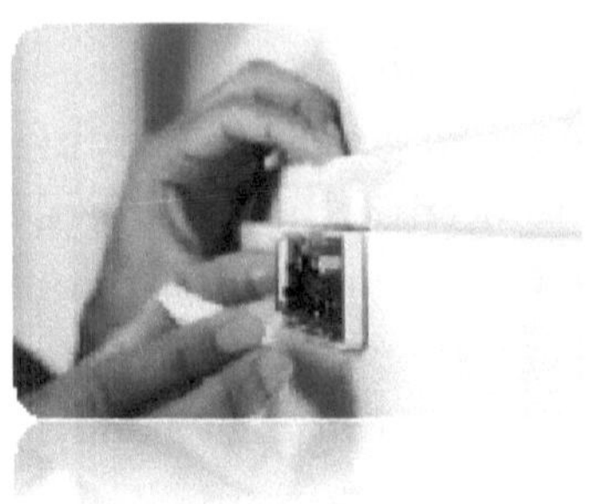

Door Sensor

E. **Status of the Aisle containment.** In case of using cold aisle or hot aisle containment, it becomes critical to monitor the aisle containment doors to make sure that they are always shut and only opened for a minimum time, to allow admins to go inside if required. It is recommended to use an automatic closing door for the aisle. The open doors might severely affect the cooling efficiency, as it allows the cold air to mix with hot air where the temperature of the servers raises and the cooling system might need more effort to cool the servers.

F. **Excess Ampere monitoring.** It is crucial to monitor the amount of energy consumption of the Datacentre, and the monitoring can be done from multiple points. For example, at the server cabinets' point, it is essential to monitor the total load on the power strips. This allows the administrator to balance the distribution of the load among the server cabinets.

Ampere Meter

It is crucial to monitor any increase in consumption to find out whether it is reasonable or caused by some unexpected issue. This monitoring prevents the sudden reach to a point where the available power is not enough for the Datacentre and might be so challenging to increase the required power in a reasonable time.

G. **Power failure monitoring.** This monitoring is similar to previous monitoring but concentrates on power failure that can be either partial or full. If it is a full failure of the primary grid, then the Automatic Transfer Switch (ATS) should start the standby generator and transfer the load to the standby generator. The grid failure needs to be monitored because the standby generator might fail to start due to an external issue such as battery failure. Also, the ATS itself can fail to work due to an internal or configuration issue; hence, this can happen at any time and the technicians need to take quick action to solve the issue. If the failure is partial such as power strip or distribution board tripping, then the technicians need to find out the cause and fix it immediately. This monitoring can be achieved via the Building Management System (BMS) and Datacentre Infrastructure Management (DCIM).

H. **Voltage fluctuations monitoring.** Voltage fluctuations can occur due to a sudden load exhibiting significant current variations. One of the symptoms of this issue is the flickering of incandescent lamps. This issue can be solved by removing the unexpected load or installing power established or Uninterruptible Power Supply (UPS) device. Fixing this problem from the roots is highly recommended because the UPS can serve critical loads such as servers and network equipment. But other equipments such as cooling units are not designed to run on UPS due to their high power requirements.

I. **Voltage imbalance monitoring.** Voltage imbalances issue appears typically due to internal issues as the equipment in the building is of two types: single-phase and three-phase. Hence, the balancing between the phases is not usually equal, especially if the electricians do not balance the distribution of the device among the three phases. The voltage in each phase of the three needs to be almost the same to avoid voltage imbalances that can cause some issues, especially for the three-phase motors (excessive heat). Therefore, it needs to be monitored and resolved as early as possible.

Voltage Meter

J. UPS battery condition monitoring. The UPS battery is very crucial for a disaster recovery plan. Therefore, it needs continuous monitoring to detect any sudden failure. Usually, UPS relies on multiple battery banks, and each bank has multiple batteries connected in series to reach the total required voltages. For example, if 120VDC is required for the UPS and each battery is 12VDC, then a total of 10 batteries is needed to be connected in series. Therefore, if one battery fails, then the whole bank stop working, which might shorten the UPS running time on power outage. Hence, monitoring the batteries is critical.

Monitoring Solutions

Building Management System (BMS)

A building management system (BMS) is a computer-based control system installed in the building. BMS controls and monitors the building's mechanical and electrical equipment such as cooling, ventilation, lighting, power systems, fire systems, and security systems. This system is highly required for the Datacentre building to keep the technicians informed about the building situation at all time.

Building Management System

DC Infrastructure Management (DCIM)

DCIM is the convergence of IT and Datacentre building facilities within the Datacentre. The goal of DCIM is to provide administrators with a clear view of the performance of the building. As a result, it is expected to achieve the best possible efficiency towards energy, equipment and floor space usage. DCIM can collect information from BMS and other mechanical and IT equipment to provide clear and easy-to-read information for the administrators. It also raises warnings when required; the administrator can refer to the Datacentre heat map provided by DCIM to choose the correct place for adding new equipment such as a new server, based on the availability of spec, power, network and cooling.

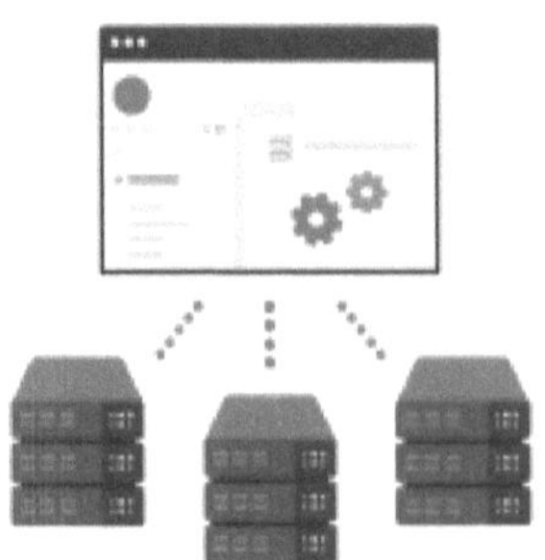

Datacentre infrastructure management

Network Operations Centre

Network Operations Centre (NOC) is a central location through which the computer network system and its communication infrastructure are controlled. Incidents of IT infrastructure are detected and resolved in this centre, and ultimately ensure that the Datacentre is working without interruption. It is worth mentioning that these problems may occur inside or outside the Datacentre. In all cases, NOC plays an essential role in coordinating and repairing these faults.

Network Operations Centre

Security Operations Centre

Security Operations Centre (SOC) is a facility that includes an information security team responsible for monitoring and analysing the security status of the Datacentre as well as the organisation on an ongoing basis. SOC specialises in all kinds of security threats, whether physical or logical. SOC employees work closely with the multi-incident response team to ensure that security issues are addressed once discovered.

Security Operations Centre

Disaster Recovery Test

Disaster Recovery Test (DR test) is the examination of every step in the disaster recovery plan, as described in the disaster recovery process of the organisation. This process is essential to ensure that the Datacentre can fully recover in the event of an actual disaster.

The following methods are the most used in the field of DRP testing:

> **Walkthrough Testing**. Although there are several monitoring systems in the Datacentre, they do not replace the human wandering. It is essential to examine the Datacentre with the naked eye as the administrator may notice an indicator for a defect or a risk that may happen for a reason or another. Thus, this must be one of the daily practice in the Datacentre.

> **Checklist Testing**. In this type of testing, the responsible team goes through the entire DR plans steps theoretically to verify the effectiveness of the recovery documentation and identify any weaknesses or gaps.

> **Simulation Testing**. In this testing, the disaster is simulated, such as power failure. The technician intentionally disconnects the grid power to see how the automated recovery works. This exercise the recovery processes and procedures. It also identifies improvements require to the DR strategy, infrastructure, and recovery processes. Usually, this test should be done monthly.

> **Business Continuity Plan.** Business Continuity Planning is highly essential for the Datacentre to guarantee the maximum Datacentre uptime. Therefore, it is created from the beginning to ensure the continuity of the Datacentre's business.

BCP PLAN HELPS TO ENSURE continued operation and service availability within the Datacentre. The above disaster recovery plan is an essential part of this plan. This plan is more comprehensive as it looks into administration parts and the steps to take to move the entire work to the disaster recovery centre smoothly and efficiently. Since this book is concerned with the design and building of Datacentres, it won't dive into BCP in details because it is a thorny topic and requires an extensive explanation.

Datacentre Cleaning Standards

The Datacentre is a controlled environment facility. Therefore, its cleanliness is highly important. It needs to be kept clean as per the standard ISO 14644-1 Class 8 or better. Class 8 allows 3.52 million 0.5μm particles per cubic meter. Class 8 is often referred to as a 5 Micron Clean or Clinical Clean. Entrance mat or sticky mats should be used for all of the white space entrances to get rid of dust from feet before entering the white space. Besides, periodic cleaning of the Datacentre must be done to get rid of dust, and a specialised company should do this task to avoid any risks.

Entrance mat

Power Usage Effectiveness (PUE)

Power usage effectiveness (PUE) is a metric used to determine the energy efficiency of the Datacentre. PUE is determined by dividing the amount of power entering the Datacentre by the power used to run the computer infrastructure within it.

$$PUE = \frac{\text{Amount of power entering a Datacentre}}{\text{Power used to run the computer infrastructure}}$$

THE TYPICAL DATACENTRE has an average PUE of 2.0 to 2.5, but it can reach 1.5 in modern Datacentre. Datacentre Infrastructure Efficiency (DCIE) is the percentage that represents the PUE and improves as it approaches 100%.

The following table displays the PUE and equivalent DCIE and level of efficiency.

PUE	DCIE	Level of Efficiency
3.0	33%	Very inefficient
2.5	40%	Inefficient
2.0	50%	Average
1.5	67%	Efficient
1.2	83%	Very Efficient

Chapter 11: Modular/Mobile Datacentres

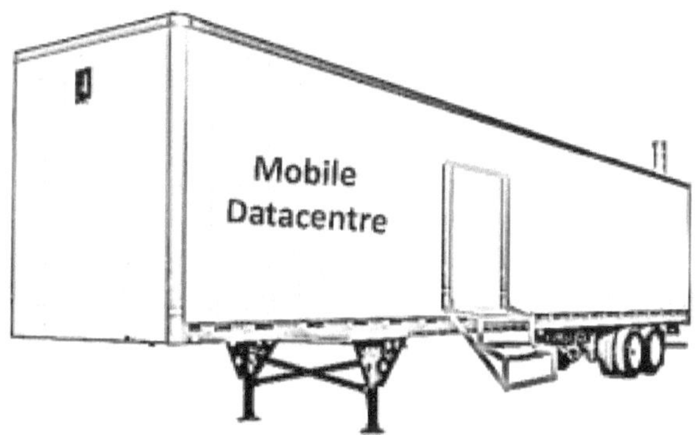

Modular Datacentres

The term modular has been mentioned several times in this book, and here we are discussing the term in details to understand what is meant by modular Datacentre.

THE IDEA BEHIND BUILDING modular Datacentre is to design a Datacentre that fulfils the current needs and guarantees future expansion without radical changes. Thus, the possibility of gradual expansion as needed is guaranteed, without a business interception or complete rebuild and at reasonable costs. This saves time, effort and money.

———◦———

FOR FLEXIBLE AND SCALABLE Datacentre, it is necessary to know the components that need to be scalable for future expansion:

1. White space.

The white space is where the server cabinets are installed and is one of the most critical components of the Datacentre. It must be wide enough to contain the required servers in the future. Due to modern cooling technologies, this space can be expanded without affecting the efficiency of the Datacentre.

White space

2. Data network room.

The data network room is a room designated for network equipment such as switches, routers and related equipment, as well as communication equipment including Private Branch Exchange (PBX) and others. Although modern designers move a lot of network equipment as a standalone cabinet and even place the top of rack distribution switches in each server cabinet to facilitate the distribution of the network, it is still essential to consider the future required space in the network room.

Data network room

3. Data network.

The data network must be designed in a way that it can be easily expanded and redundancy should be considered from the beginning such that if one of the lines fails, the alternate line should take its place. Moreover, load balancing needs to be considered. All network pieces of equipment need to have alternatives that automatically take the service load.

4. Electricity system

a. **Power grid.** Reliable power grids are essential for the Datacentre. It is necessary to obtain electricity supply from two independent networks if the Datacentre is designed to be Tier4 Datacentre, according to Uptime Institutes. Some designers might be lenient in this regard because of the difficulty of achieving this in some countries and its high costs, and they consider reliable backup generators as an alternative to the second grid. However, this constitutes a barrier to obtaining a real Tier 4 Datacentre.

Interconnected electric network delivering electricity from producers to consumer

b. **Transformer.** An electrical transformer is a passive electrical device that transfers electrical energy from one electrical circuit to another. It transfers the High Voltage (HV) to Low Voltage (LV). LV is the standard voltage that is used to run appliances. It is usually 120VAC (US) or 230VAC (UK). Typically, you need two sets of transformers, one for each grid or both connected to the same grid in Tier 3 datacentres. Always design the system to accept a higher capacity transformer in future upgrading or add another transformer supporting the first transformer to raise the total energy with minimum effort and cost.

Transformer

c. **Standby Generators.** Standby generator capacity is decided based on the cumulative load required by the Datacentre. For Tier 4, it is required to have dual standby generators. It is highly recommended to prepare the electrical connectivity and switchboards for a future upgrade based on the Datacentre equipment expansion. The synchronisation panel needs to be designed from the beginning to accept the addition of new standby generators, as this facilitates the future upgrade process. The required space for the synchronisation panel expansion, the generators and fuel tanks should also be considered from the beginning.

Standby Generator

d. **Uninterruptible Power Supply (UPS).** It is one of the essential systems in the Datacentre. And typically, there are two sets of UPS designed to withstand the current Datacentre load with some safety margin. It is crucial to use modular UPS that accepts load capacity expansion and running time expansion with ease rather than the conventional type. Please note that there is a limit for the maximum allowed expansion of each UPS unit; you might need to add another unit if you reach the maximum limit. For example, if the current load requires 300KVA, it is better to install a UPS with a maximum of 500KVA, where the initial install modules are 300KVA only. With this, the chassis can still accept 200KVA before the need to install another parallel UPS. In all cases, always keep an extra space for extra UPS in the room just in case and keep more space in the battery room in case you need to extend the running time or add new batteries to accommodate the expansion in the UPS load.

UPS

e. **Switchboards.** Switchboards are also needed to be designed in a way that it can be upgraded and should keep enough space in the room to add more boards.

Switchboard

f. **Internal power distribution**. The internal power distribution needs to be modular; therefore, it is recommended to go with Bus-bar system rather than the conventional system based on Remote Power Panel (RPP) and flexible cable. Future expansion is straightforward with Bus-bar system as you only need to add the required Tap-off box. But for the conventional way, you need to add two flexible cables, industrial female connectors and isolator switches, and if the RPP is full, then you need to install a new RPP and a new main cable from the switchboard.

Distribution board

5. Cooling

a. **Chillers**. If chillers are used for Datacentre cooling, then it should be a modular type where the required capacity is to be installed. It is also possible to add more modules to expand the chiller capacity in future. It is highly essential to consider having modulation for all other related components.

Cooling tower

b. **Outdoor units.** For DX cooling, the outdoor units are either installed on the roof of the Datacentre or in the back yard of the Datacentre, which is better. In all cases, there should be enough area for future outdoor units and full ducts for fragrant lines.

DX outdoor units

c. **Computer room air conditioning (CRAC)** units. The allocated space for CRAC units should be able to accommodate the expected devices for future expansion. In the beginning, the required CRACs are to be installed only, and the rest space should be used for future expansion.

CRAC Unit

6. Network topology.

The network in the Datacentre must support future expansion and should be designed as fault tolerance, which means that in case of failure of any device such as a router or switch, another device should be available to take over.

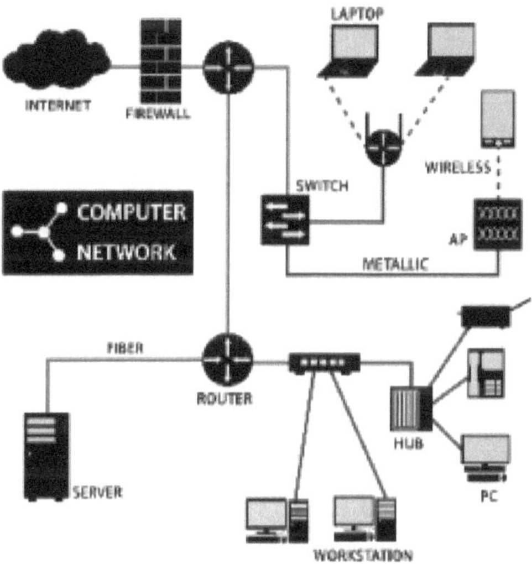

Network topology

Container Datacentre

In some situations, there might be a need to build a Datacentre urgently to serve some sudden requirements or maybe a company tend to reduce the total cost. In this situation, the company has a choice to use a container Datacentre, which is usually portable and can be deployed anywhere and in a short time.

CONTAINER DATACENTRES are made up of modules that are purpose-engineered. It can be in one or more container joined together to become a large Datacentre. Initially, one container can come with a standby generator, cooling unit, data network, server cabinets and safety and security systems. If the container Datacentre is ready to be plugged into external electricity power and network source, then it is ready to go.

IT IS POSSIBLE TO ALLOCATE a covered backyard for these containers. With this, it becomes a reliable working Datacentre which can serve any requirements.

Portable Datacentre

The Portable Modular Datacentre is a portable Datacentre solution built into a standard 20, 40, or 53-foot intermodal container. It contains all of the Datacentre facility requirements. The main difference between portable Datacentre and container Datacentre is that the portable Datacentre is designed to be portable, where you can move it from one place to another with ease. It can be moved anywhere as a standalone infrastructure. This Datacentre is useful for military and security purposes. The large companies can also use it for some extra-large projects..

Chapter 12: Datacentre Standards

Are Standards Important?

Standards are created to help designers follow a few steps that previous experts have put in place, and this makes the design process more comfortable and more accurate. The following are some of the standards that help the designer to design a Datacentre properly; the designer can choose the standard that suits the country and the environment. Always put in mind that the standards are a guide for a better result, and the best standard is something that best suits your needs.

REQUIREMENTS
REGULATIONS
POLICIES
COMPLIANCE
RULES
LAW
STANDARDS
TRANSPARENCY

TIA/EIA-568-A-1995

Commercial Building Telecommunications Wiring Standards. It defines the technical and performance criteria for cabling. It also defines the standard for building a cable system for buildings that supports data networks, voice, and video.

ANSI/TIA-942-A Infrastructure Standard for Datacentre

This North American standard references the TIA-568 series of the standards but contains additional information appropriate for Datacentres.

⬦ Outlines the Datacentre specific functional areas.
⬦ Provides minimum recommendations for pathways and spaces.
⬦ Backbone and horizontal cable media distances.
⬦ Redundancy.
⬦ Cable management and environmental considerations.

ANSI/BICSI 002-2014 Datacentre Design and Implementation Best Practices

This standard is a Datacentre design and operation guide that covers:

Planning.
Construction.
Commissioning.
Protection.
Management.

Maintenance of Datacentre.
Cabling infrastructure.
Pathways and spaces.
Modular and container Datacentres.
Energy efficiency.

CENELEC EN 50173-5 Information Technology

Generic Cabling Systems Part 5 for Datacentres. Harmonized with TIA-942, this European Union (EU) Standard specifies requirements for cabling within Datacentres to support existing and emerging applications.

ISO/IEC 24764 Information Technology

G eneric Cabling Systems for Datacentres - Based on both TIA-942 and EN 50173-5, this is the international standard that specifies cabling to use within the Datacentre.

It references the cabling requirements of ISO/IEC 11801 with additional information pertinent to Datacentres.

Uptime Institute

This is an advisory organisation that provides guidelines for improving the performance, efficiency and reliability of critical Datacentre infrastructure.

1. The Uptime Institute established the Tier Classification System to define Datacentre availability.

2. Tier I provides basic capacity.

3. Tier II provides redundant capacity.

4. Tier III is considered concurrently maintainable with no shutdowns for maintenance.

5. Tier IV being fault-tolerant with a 99.99% availability level.

6. Each Tier level includes the average annual allowable hours of downtime.

Uptime Institute

ASHRAE 90.4-2016

This standard contains recommendations for:

- ◈ The design.
- ◈ Construction.
- ◈ Operation.
- ◈ Maintenance of Datacentres.

Moreover, this standard focuses on the use of both on-site and off-site renewable energy and provides thermal guidelines that recommend cooling best practices and temperature ranges that help ensure reliability and efficiency.

The Green Grid

This is non-profit, open industry association of end-users.

- Policymakers.
- Technology providers.
- Facility architects.

This association is also credited with the development of Power Usage Effectiveness (PUE), a method of measuring energy efficiency in Datacentres that compares all the energy consumed in the Datacentre to those consumed by the active equipment.

TIP : *Even though the standards are essential when designing and building a Datacentre, put in mind that these standards are set based on the minimum requirements and is always said that the best standard is the standard that suits your needs at a specific time and place.*

Conclusion

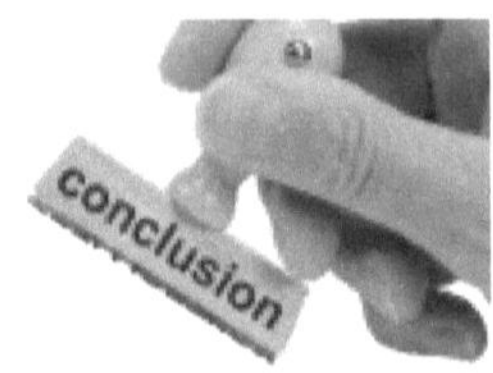

I HOPE THAT I HAVE succeeded in covering the majority of the points that must be taken into account when designing and building Datacentres. I would also like to point out that Datacentre's science continues to evolve, just as other information technology science. Therefore, specialists must continue to follow the developments in this field to ensure that they have the latest knowledge reached in the field.

I hope to be able to publish another book that specialises in the management and maintenance of Datacentres, which will cover in-depth in terms of disaster recovery and business continuity.

I would also like to express my appreciation to you my dear reader for your interest in obtaining and reading this book. I hope that it adds some knowledge to you in the field of Datacentres.

Glossary

Colocation (COLO): It is a term describing leasing space, power and bandwidth from a Datacentre provider.

Big Data: It is a term used to describe the large volume of data, whether structured or unstructured, that floods business on a daily basis.

Software as a service (SaaS): It is a software distribution model in which a third-party provider hosts applications and makes them available to prospective customers over the internet.

Platform-as-a-Service (PaaS): It is a cloud-computing model in which cloud vendors provide developers with a platform for building apps.

Infrastructure as a service (IaaS): It is a form of cloud computing that provides virtualised computing resources over the internet.

Desktop as a Service (DaaS): It is a form of cloud computing service where the service provider provides a virtual desktop to end-users over the internet.

Recovery Time Objective (RTO): It represents the amount of time a service can be disrupted and not result in significant damage to businesses and the time it takes for the service to come back.

Recovery Point Objective (RPO): It describes the period of time during which an organisation operation must be restored after a disruptive event.

Electromagnetic compatibility (EMC): Electromagnetic compatibility is the extent to which electrical equipment and systems are able to function reasonably well in a particular electromagnetic environment.

Ring Main Unit (RMU): In an electrical power distribution system, the ring main unit is a factory assembled, metal-enclosed switchgear used at the load connection points of a circuit distribution network.

Diesel Generator (DG): A diesel generator is a combination of a diesel engine and an electric generator to generate electric power.

Automatic Transfer Switch (ATS): It is a self-acting intelligent power switch that is governed by the custom control logic. When the connected power supply fails, the ATS automatically send a signal to the generator to start and transfers the load circuit to the active power supply.

Static Transfer Switch (STS): It is an intelligent switch that automatically transfers loads to alternative power sources in no time when the primary power source fails.

UPS: Uninterruptible power supply is an electrical device that provides emergency power to a load when the main power supply is cut off.

Direct current (DC): It is the one-directional or unidirectional flow electric charge.

Alternating current(AC): An alternating current is an electrical current that periodically reverses its direction and continuously changes its size over time.

High Voltage (HV): Electricity is generally classified as high voltage (HV) if it exceeds 1,000 Volt AC or 1,500 Volt DC.

Low voltage (LV): Low-voltage electricity means electrical power with voltages over 32 Volt AC or 115 Volt DC, and less than 1000 Volt AC or 1500 Volt DC.

Volt-amps (VA): A volt-ampere (VA) is a measure of the apparent electrical power while an amp (A) is a measure of electrical current.

Remote Power Panel (RPP): It is also called **"Floor Mount Power Distribution Unit (FMPDU)."** It provides power distribution extensions from main switchboards or other power sources directly to the power strips or the PDU in the server racks.

Power Distribution Units (PDU): It is a device fitted within the servers rack and equipped with multiple power outputs designed to facilitate the electric power distribution to the servers and networking equipment located within the rack.

Emergency Power Off (EPO): It is a control mechanism, which aims to shut down a piece of electronic equipment or even the whole of the Datacentre. This system is usually located in the Datacentre to be used in emergency situations such as fire. It is also available next to the backup generator to turn it off directly in emergency cases.

Signal Reference Grid (SRG): It is a means to reduce high-frequency impedance which is the so-called noise. It is a standard ground reference for all connected equipment in the Datacentre. The grid has multiple paths to ground.

Kilo-volt-amperes (KVA): A KVA is 1,000 volt-amps. It is a result of multiplying the voltage by the amps.

Kilowatt (KW): It is merely 1,000 watts. It equals multiplying the voltage by the full-load current.

Power Usage Effectiveness (PUE): Energy efficiency is a ratio that describes how efficiently a Datacentre uses energy. Specifically, it is the amount of energy the computing equipment uses compared to the total energy consumed.

Datacentre infrastructure efficiency (DCIE): It is a performance improvement measure used to calculate the energy efficiency of a Datacentre. It is the percentage value derived by dividing the power of the IT equipment by the total power of the Datacentre.

Heating, ventilation, and air conditioning (HVAC): It is the technology for controlling the indoor environmental comfort for buildings.

Cold-aisle/Hot-aisle containment: It is the hot and cold airstreams separated to avoid mixing of hot and cold air; this is highly important for extreme efficiency.

Direct Expansion (DX): A direct expansion air conditioning unit cools indoor air using a special condenser refrigerant liquid.

Chilled water cooling system (Schiller): Chilled water systems provide cooling to extensive facilities by using chilled water to absorb heat from building spaces.

Computer room air conditioning (CRAC): A Datacentre air conditioning unit is a device that monitors and maintains the temperature, air and humidity distribution in a Datacentre.

Relative humidity (rH): The relative humidity is the ratio of the partial pressure of water vapour to the equilibrium water vapour pressure at a given temperature.

(μm): Called micrometre by international spelling. It is used as weights and measures, also commonly known as a micron.

National Fire Protection Association (NFPA): It is an international nonprofit organisation devoted to eliminating injury death, property and economic loss due to electrical, fire and related hazards.

Very Early Smoke Detection Apparatus (VESDA): It is a system that detects smoke. It is used in early warning applications where fire response is critical, such as Datacentre. It works by continuously drawing air from Datacentre into the piping system through a highly efficient extractor hood. Then a sample of that air is passed through a two-stage filter to detect any impurities in the air, which may be an indication of the imminent outbreak of a fire.

Closed-circuit television (CCTV): Closed-circuit television, also known as video surveillance, is the use of video cameras to transmit video to a specific location, on a set of screens.

Infrared light for night vision (IR): Infrared light has longer wavelengths than visible light. Infrared ray is invisible to the human eye, and for night vision devices, it works as an infrared flashlight.

Pound (lbs): Pound is a unit of mass, each pound is equal to 0.453592 kilogram.

Epoxy coating: It is a coating compound consisting of two elements (epoxy resin and a polyamine hardener). Epoxy coatings provide optimum protection against turbulence, corrosive fluids, abrasion, and extreme temperatures.

KiloNewton (KN): The newton is the International System of Units derived unit of force. One kilonewton is equivalent to about 100kg of load under Earth gravity.

Building Management System (BMS): It is a system that is sometimes known as a "building automation system." It is a computer-based control system that is installed in buildings to control and monitor the buildings electrical and mechanical equipment such as ventilation, power systems, lighting, fire and security systems.

Datacentre Infrastructure Management System (DCIM): It is a system that monitors the Datacentre; its goal is to provide administrators with a holistic view of the status of the Datacentre performance so that the resources such as energy, equipment and floor space are used as efficiently as possible.

Integrated Lights-Out (ILO): It is a proprietary embedded server management technology by Hewlett-Packard which provides advanced server management facilities.

Intelligent Infrastructure Management (IIM): It is a solution to provide the missing link between real-time network management tools and the ordinary passive structured cabling infrastructures that normally connect network devices.

Radio Frequency Identification (RFID): Radiofrequency uses electromagnetic fields to identify and track signs attached to an object.

RFID tag usually consists of a small radio device; a transmitter and a receiver.

Normally Open (NO): In (NO) devices such as rim lock or strike lock, when voltage is applied to the relay/contactor terminals, this contact opens, and the lock opens.

Normally Closed (NC): In NC devices, such as electromagnetic locks, when voltage is applied to the relay/contactor terminals, this contact closes, and the lock closes.

Network Video Recorder (NVR): A network video recorder is a specialised computer system that includes special software that records video to a drive or any mass storage device.

Serial Advanced Technology Attachment (SATA): It is a standard for connecting and transferring data from hard disk drives to computer systems or network video recorder. As its name implies, SATA is based on serial signalling technology, unlike Integrated Drive Electronics hard drives that use parallel signalling.

Storage Area Network (SAN): It is a computer network device that provides access to consolidated, block-level data storage. It is primarily used to access storage devices, such as disk arrays from servers. The devices appear to the operating system as inbuilt direct-attached storage.

Network-Attached Storage (NAS): It is a file-level computer data storage server connected to a computer network providing data access to clients. It is specialised for serving files where clients can access specific shared folders based on the preset authorisations.

Small Computer System Interface (SCSI): It is a set of standards for physically connecting and transferring data between computers and peripheral devices. These standards define commands, electrical, protocols, optical and logical interfaces.

Redundant Array of Inexpensive Disks (RAID): It is a data storage virtualisation technology that combines multiple physical disk drive into one or more logical units for performance improvement and data redundancy.

Pan-tilt-zoom (PTZ) camera: It is a camera that is capable of changing directionally to all directions, zoom and focus remotely.

Wide Dynamic Range (WDR): Wide Dynamic Range is a term used in the CCTV industry to refer to the camera that can handle bright and dark conditions to improve the quality of the image.

Network Operations Centre (NOC): It is also known as a network management centre. It is a location where the network is monitored, controlled, or managed, through a computer system.

Security Operations Centre (SOC): It is a central location that deals with security issues on an organisational and technical level where staff supervises and monitor the physical and logical security issues, using data processing technology.

Private Branch Exchange (PBX): It is a multiline telephone system typically used in business environments, encompassing systems ranging in technology from the legacy key telephone system to an IP based key telephone system.

Disaster Recovery Plan (DRP): Disaster recovery includes a set of plans, policies, tools and procedures developed to enable the restoration or continuation of vital technical infrastructure and systems in the aftermath of a disaster, whether it is a natural or man-made disaster.

Disaster Recovery Test (DR test): It is a multi-step drill for an enterprise disaster recovery plan, designed to ensure that the IT system is restored in the event of an actual disaster.

Capital Expenditure (CAPEX): It is the major, long-term expenses such as buying a device or system.

Operational Expenditure (OPEX): Is a day-to-day expense spent on maintaining a device or system.

Black start: It is the process of restoring an electric power without relying on an external electric power source.

About the Author

ENGINEER SAID AL HOSNI has vast experience in the field of information technology including information systems management, IT infrastructure planning, Datacentre design, IT audit, implementation management, as well as operation.

Academic degrees such as Bachelor of Engineering in Data Communication and Systems Administration, and Master of Science in Information Systems from the venerable University of Coventry, UK, along with professional certificates such as Certified Datacentre Management Professional (CDCMP), Certified Datacentre Audit Professional (CDCAP), and Certified Datacentre Design Professional (CDCDP).

He becomes a valued Consultant to various institutions due to passing through multiple stages, and the extensive experience gained in numerous areas, e.g., hardware, software and Datacentre infrastructure planning, implementation and management.

He was recently appointed as an information systems expert accredited to the Ministry of Justice and law affairs.

He has successfully led and delivered multiple Datacentre projects against deadlines and budgets, assessing and identifying risks and determining corrective action and solutions.

Don't miss out!

Visit the website below and you can sign up to receive emails whenever Engineer Said AL Hosni publishes a new book. There's no charge and no obligation.

https://books2read.com/r/B-A-COKM-IVCKB

Connecting independent readers to independent writers.

About the Author

Engineer Said AL Hosni has vast experience in the field of information technology including information systems management, IT infrastructure planning, Datacentre design, IT audit, implementation management, as well as operation.

Academic degrees such as Bachelor of Engineering in Data Communication and Systems Administration, and Master of Science in Information Systems from the venerable University of Coventry, UK, along with professional certificates such as Certified Datacentre Management Professional (CDCMP), Certified Datacentre Audit Professional (CDCAP), and Certified Datacentre Design Professional (CDCDP).

He becomes a valued Consultant to various institutions due to passing through multiple stages, and the extensive experience gained in numerous areas, e.g., hardware, software and Datacentre infrastructure planning, implementation and management.